About Plastic Lace

• Flat lace has been around for decades. It is available in almost every color, including glow-in-the-dark and glitter.

• Flat lace is especially good for projects which require a lot of braiding. It also makes tighter, longer-lasting curls.

• Always make sure you start with enough lace. It is harder to handle long strands when beginning to braid, but it is more difficult when you run out of lace and need to add more to finish the project.

• If you need to keep track of which strand is which, tape a label to the end of each strand.

• Always pull the knot or braid as tightly as you can. Pull lace until it stretches slightly — that's how you know it's right.

• If you need to leave a project before it's finished, use an office clip to hold your place.

• When braiding or wrapping with flat lace, take care to keep the strands from twisting.

• Use Jewelry Glue to seal knots when needed.

• Cut lace at an angle to make it easier to string beads. If inserting more than one strand through a bead, push through one at a time. Pony beads have large holes which will hold several strands of lace.

Easy Wrap Bead Necklace

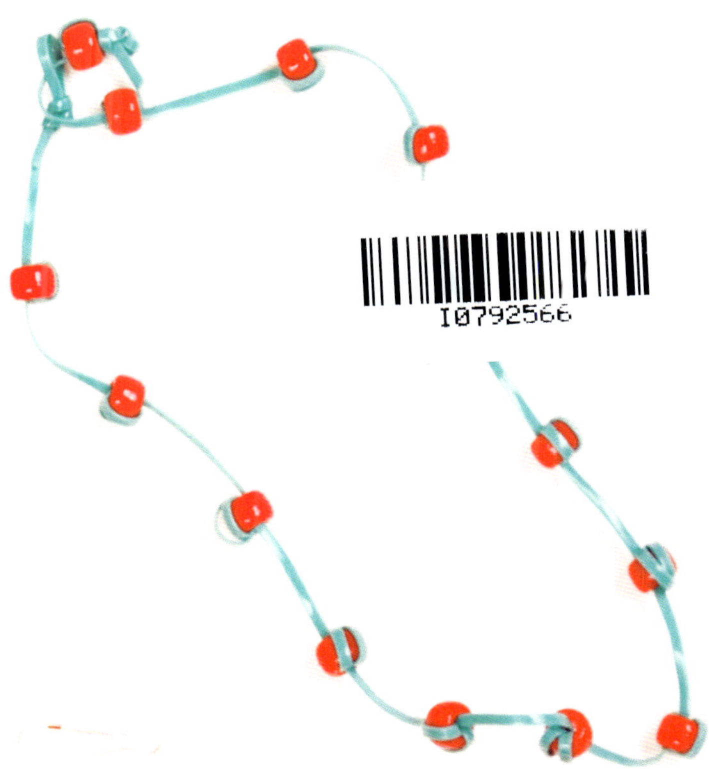

SIZE: necklace 18" or bracelet 9"

MATERIALS:
Plastic $\frac{1}{8}$" flat craft lace
(necklace 48" of Color A-Turquoise, or bracelet 30" of Color A)
Pony beads (necklace 14, bracelet 7)
Tape or Safety pin • Lanyard hook or paper clip

INSTRUCTIONS:

Knot 3 Overhand knots, one on top of the other to make a large tight knot on one end of the lace. Thread a bead onto lace and push it all the way to the knot. Pass lace through the bead 2 more times keeping the lace tight. This first bead serves as the clasp.

Thread the next bead leaving a 1" space. Continue until necklace or bracelet is the desired length.

Tie a loop in the end large enough to slip over the clasp bead.

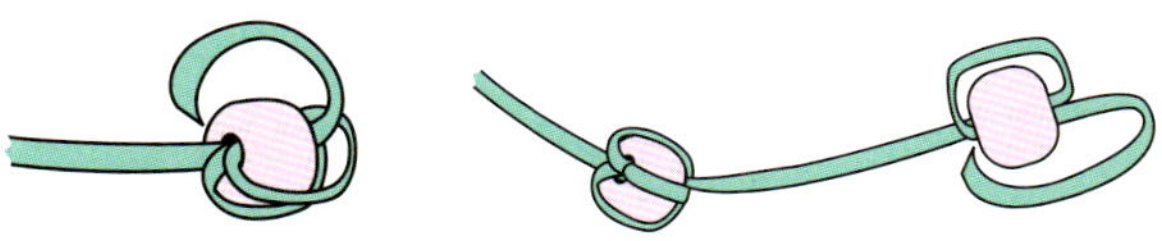

Thread lace through pony bead 3 times keeping the lace tight. Leave a space between the beads and repeat.

Double Wrap Bead Necklace

SIZE: 9"

MATERIALS:
Plastic $\frac{1}{8}$" flat craft lace (30" Color A-Red, 24" Color B-Blue)
Tape or Safety pin • Lanyard hook or paper clip

INSTRUCTIONS:

Fold one end of both strands over at 4". Tie an Overhand knot $\frac{1}{2}$" from the fold. Thread a bead onto both laces and push it all the way to the knot. Pass Color A-Red lace through the bead 2 more times keeping the lace tight. This first bead serves as the clasp.

Thread the next bead leaving a 1" space. Continue until bracelet is the desired length.

Tie a loop in the end large enough to slip over the clasp bead.

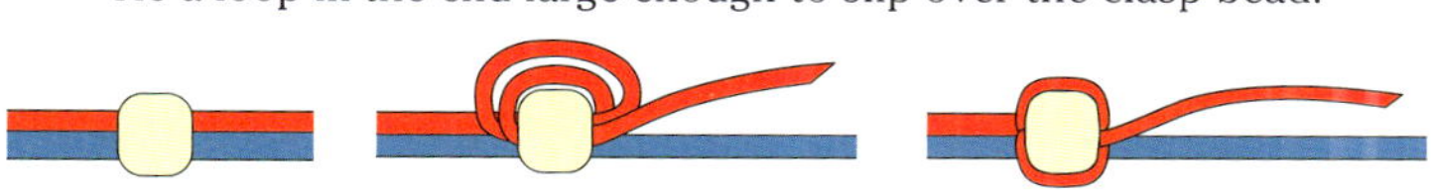

Thread 2 strands into bead.
Pass the end of 1 strand (Color A-Red) back into the bead twice.
Pass the second strand back through the bead once and pull tight.

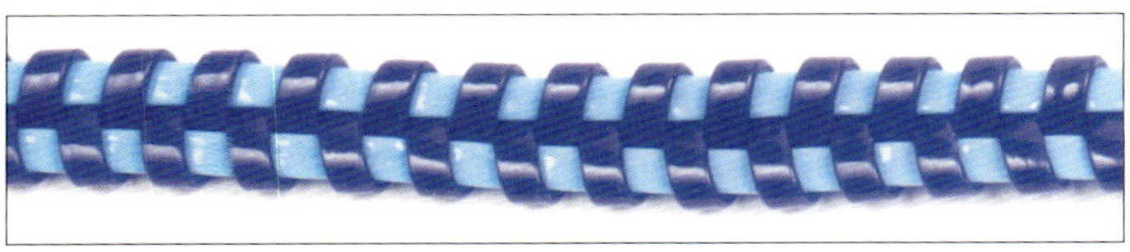

Zipper Braid

SIZE: 9"

MATERIALS for Bracelet:

Plastic $^1/_8$" flat craft lace (24" of Color A-Blue, 48" of Color B-Dark Blue)
Tape or Safety pin • Lanyard hook or paper clip

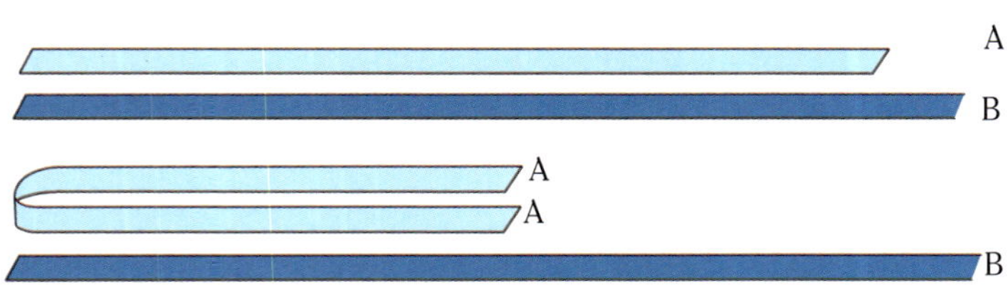

1. Label the short lace "A" and the long lace "B". Fold lace A in half and stack the laces together.

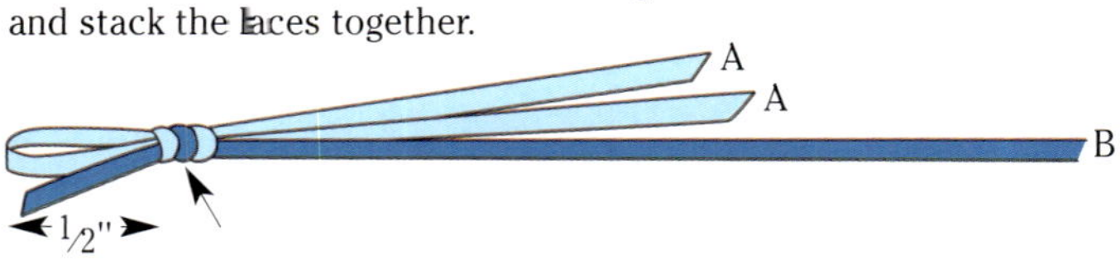

2. Tie an Overhand knot $^1/_2$" from the fold.
   Attach a hook or paper clip to the fold.

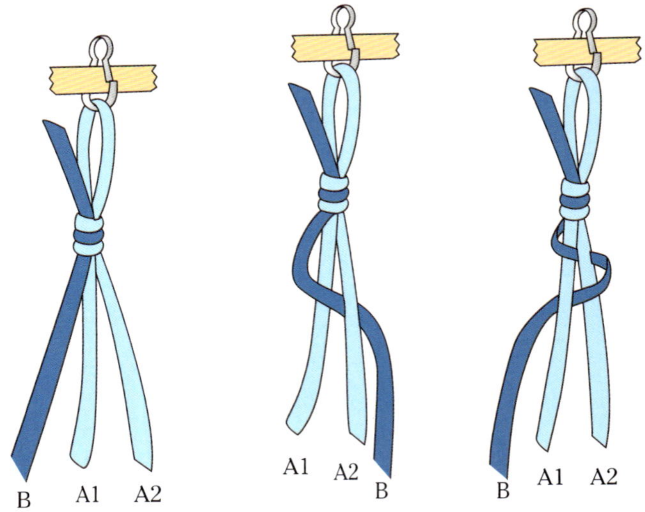

3. Tape or pin the hook to a surface to make it easier to braid.
   Hold the A strands straight like railroad tracks and keep the B strand flat as you weave.
   Bring B between the tracks, around A2, between the tracks and around A1.

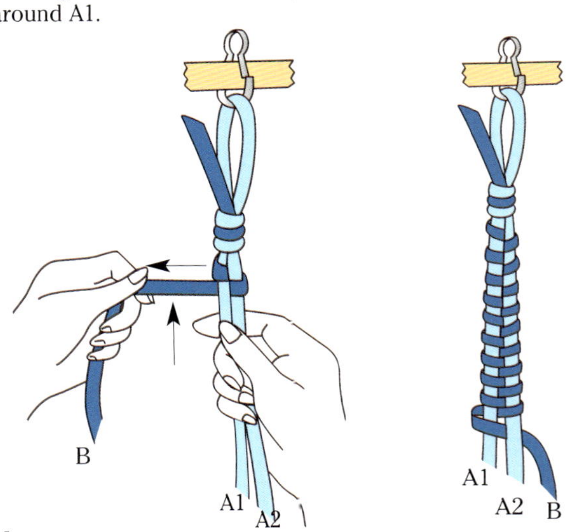

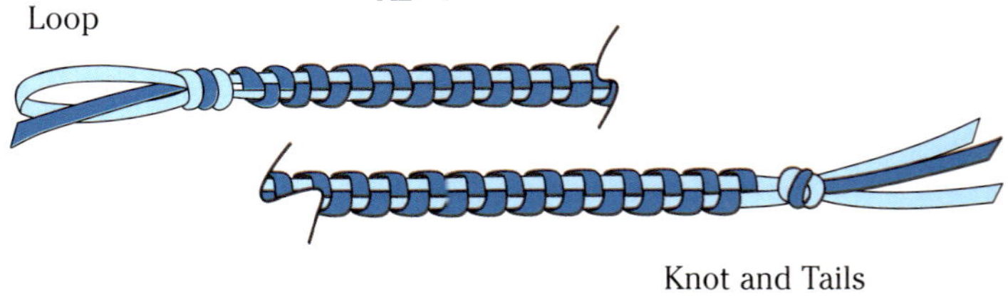

4. Slide the stitches together snugly as you weave.
   Continue until the bracelet fits your wrist.
5. Remove the tape and hook from the loop end of the bracelet.
   Tie 2 Overhand knots, one on top of the other. Trim the tails.

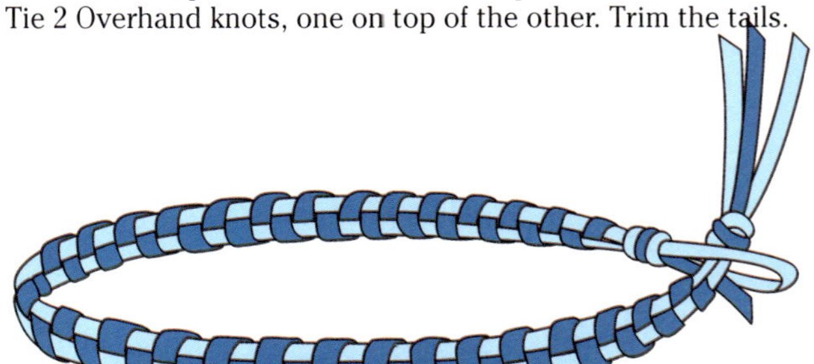

6. Wrap bracelet around your wrist and slide the knot into the loop.

KEYCHAIN: (12" of Color A-Blue, 24" of Color B-Dark Blue) Make a Zipper keychain by making the braid shorter and leaving the hook in place.

Corkscrew Braid

SIZE: 9"

MATERIALS for Bracelet:
Plastic 1/8" craft lace (48" of Color A-Pink, 48" of Color B-White)
Tape • Paper clip or Safety pin

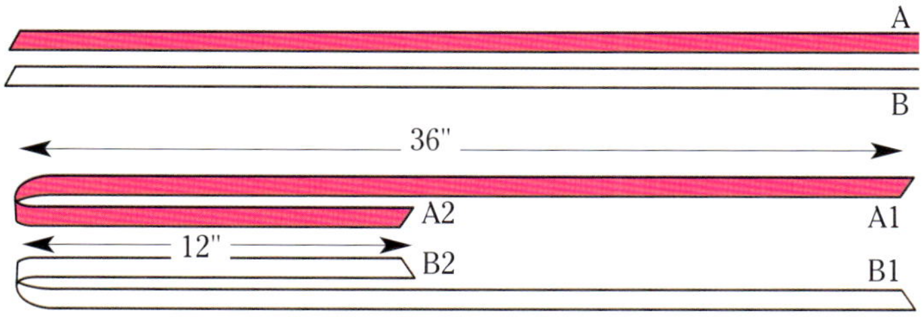

1. Fold each lace 12" from the end.

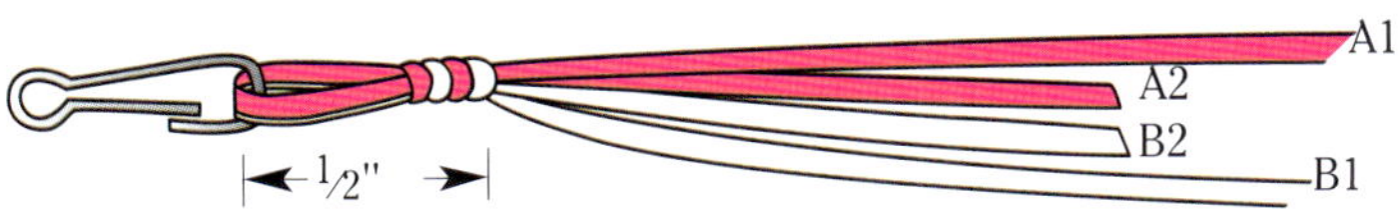

2. Tie an Overhand knot 1/2" from the fold. Attach a hook or paper clip to the fold.

3. Tape or pin the hook to a surface to make it easier to braid.
Position the short strands in the center and the long strands on the outside.
4. Bring A1 OVER both short strands forming a loop.
Go UNDER B1. Let go of A1.
5. Bring B1 UNDER both short strands and UP through the loop.
6. Keeping the laces flat, pull the long strands tight to form a knot.

7. Bring B1 OVER the short strands forming a loop.
Go UNDER A1.

3

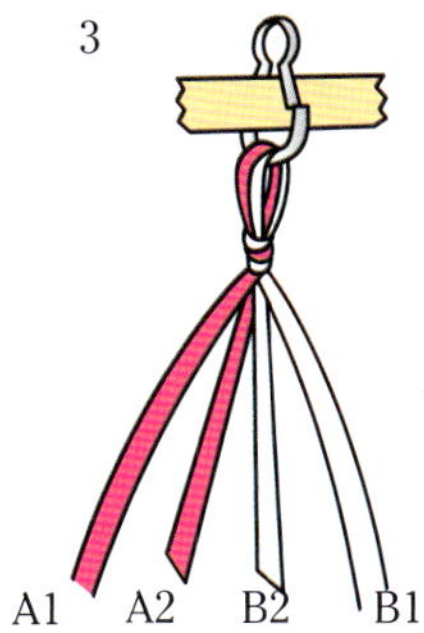

4

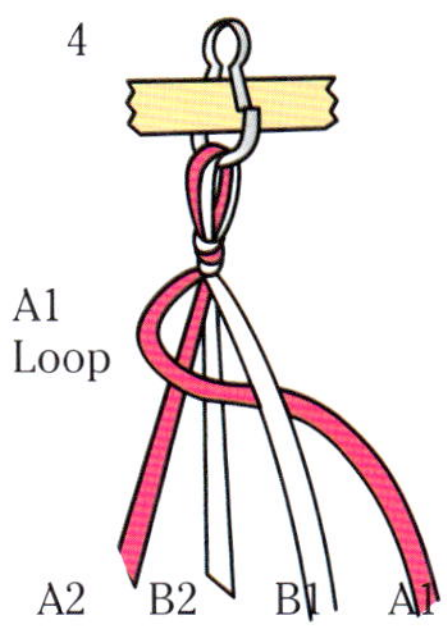

5

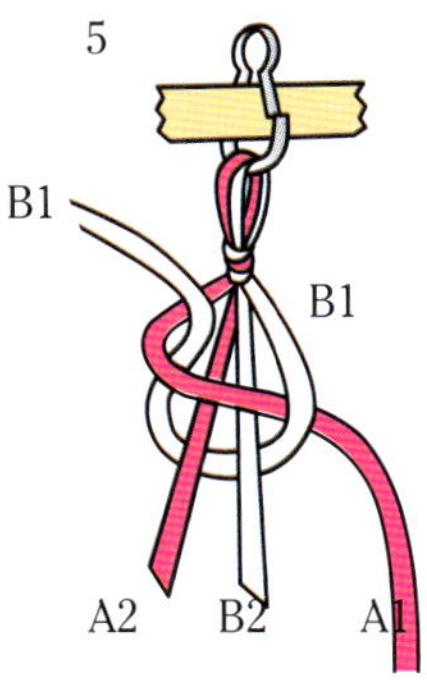

6

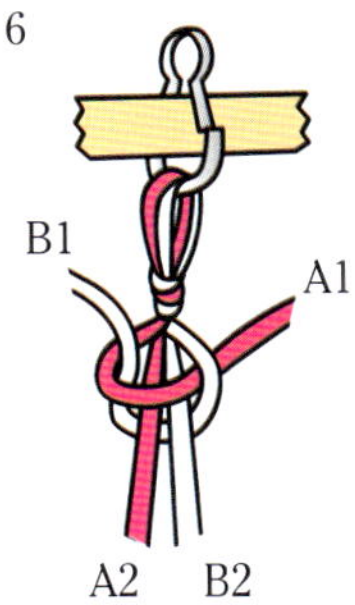

7

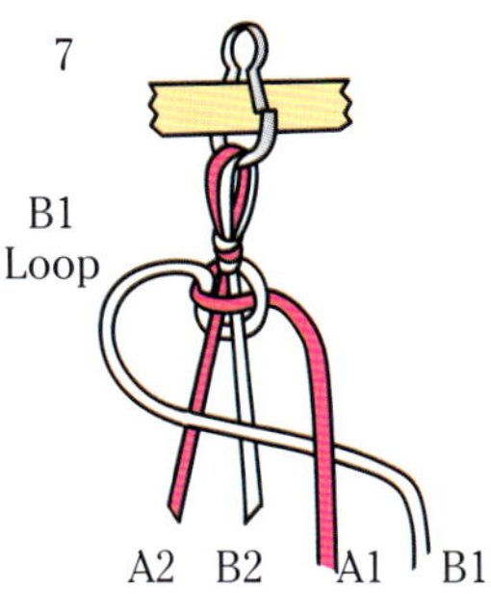

8

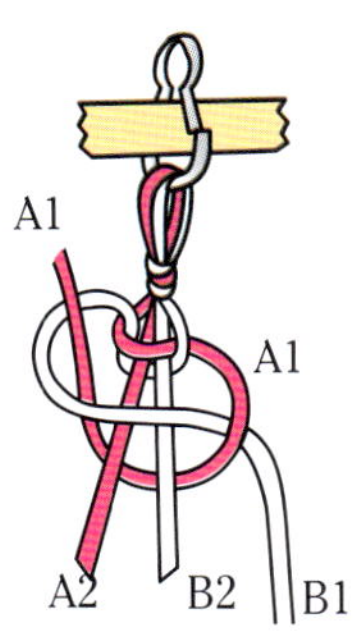

9

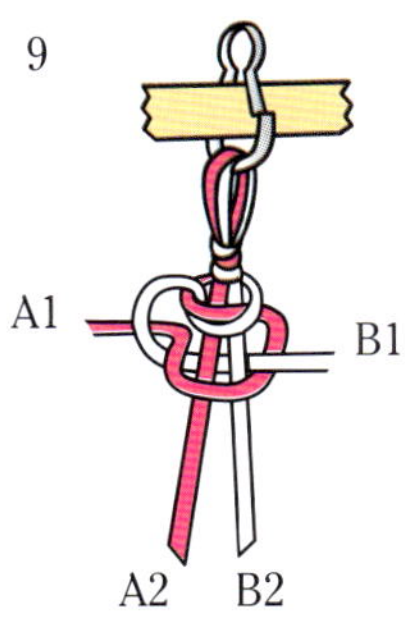

8. Bring A1 UNDER the short strands and UP through the loop.
9. Keeping the laces flat, pull the long strands to form a knot.
Repeat steps 4 - 9 until the bracelet fits your wrist.

10. Remove the hook from the loop end of the bracelet.
Tie 2 Overhand knots, one on top of the other. Trim the tails.
11. Wrap bracelet around your wrist and slide the knot into the loop.

KEYCHAIN: (24" of Color A-Pink, 24" of Color B-White) Make a Corkscrew keychain by making the braid shorter and leaving the hook in place.

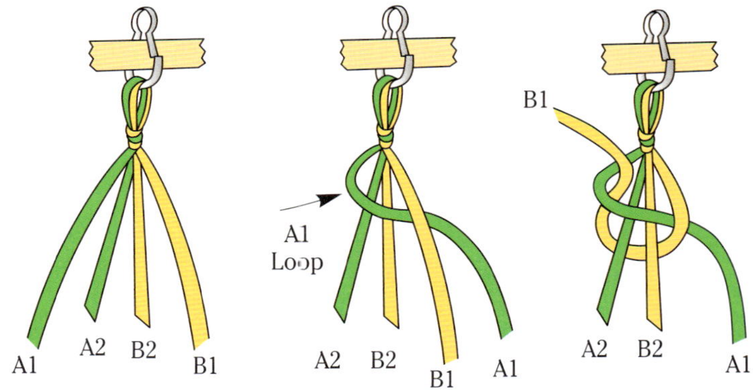

3. Tape or pin the hook to a surface to make it easier to braid. Position short strands in the center, long strands on the outside.
4. Bring A1 OVER both short strands forming a loop. Go UNDER B1. Let go of A1.
5. Pick up B1, bring it UNDER both short strands and UP through the loop.

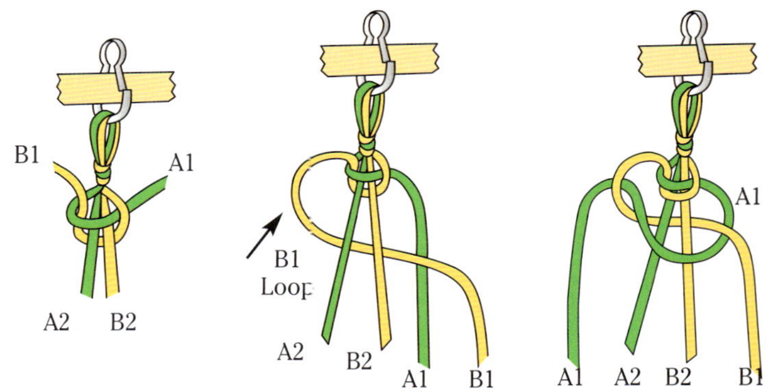

6. Tighten the knot by pulling both long strands.
7. Form a loop with B1, bringing it UNDER the short strands and OVER A1.
8. Bring A1 OVER both short strands and DOWN through the loop.

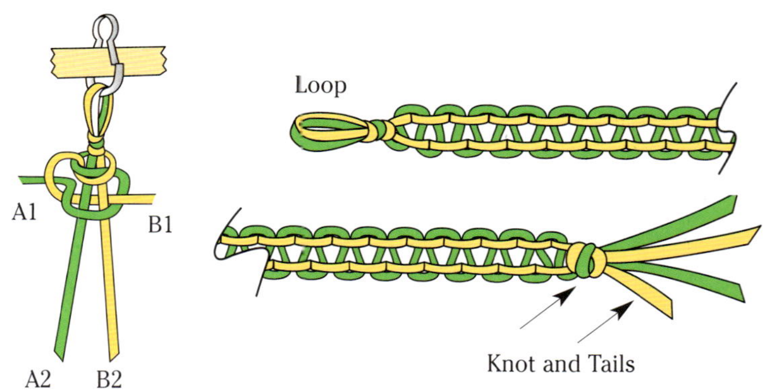

9. Keeping the laces flat, pull the long strands to form a knot. Repeat steps 4 - 9 until the bracelet fits your wrist.
10. Remove the hook from the loop end of the bracelet. Tie 2 Overhand knots, one on top of the other. Trim the tails.

11. Wrap bracelet around your wrist and slide the knot into the loop.

KEYCHAIN: (24" of Color A-Green, 24" of Color B-Yellow) Make a Ladder keychain by making the braid shorter and leaving the hook in place.

Ladder Braid

SIZE: 9"

MATERIALS for Bracelet:

Plastic 1/8" flat craft lace (48" of Color A-Green, 48" of Color B-Yellow)
Tape or Safety pin • Lanyard hook or paper clip

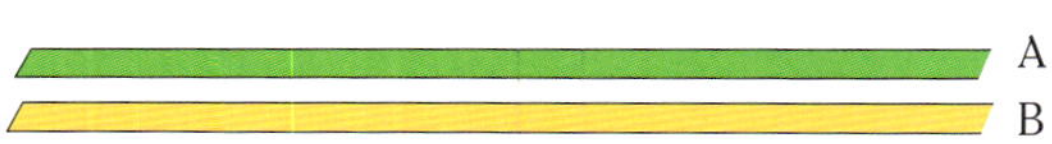

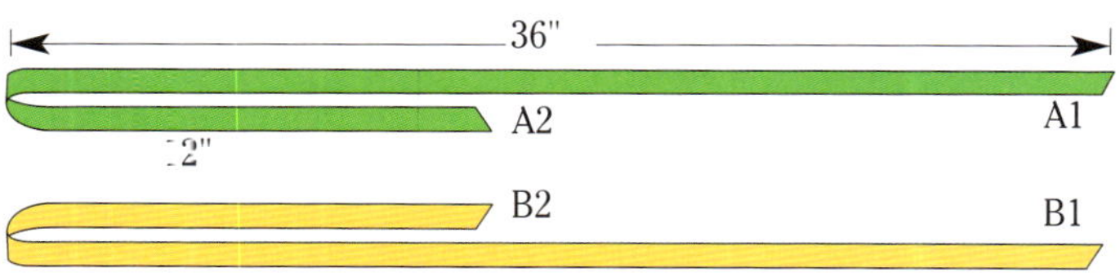

1. Fold each lace 12" from the end.

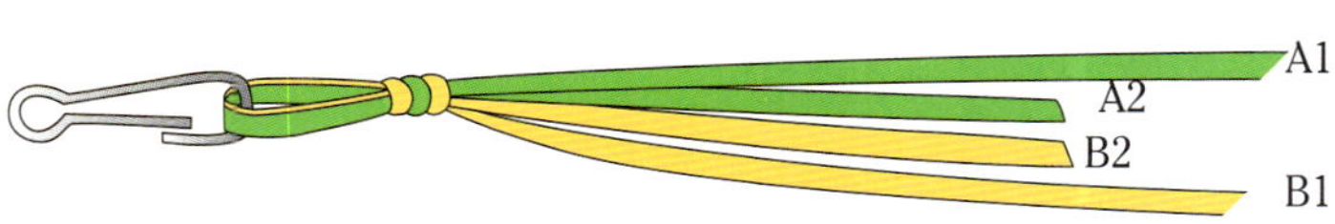

2. Attach a hook or paper clip to the fold. Tie an Overhand knot 1/2" from the fold.

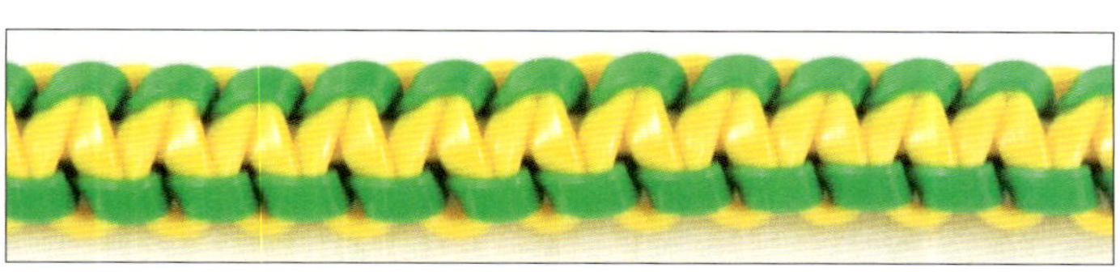

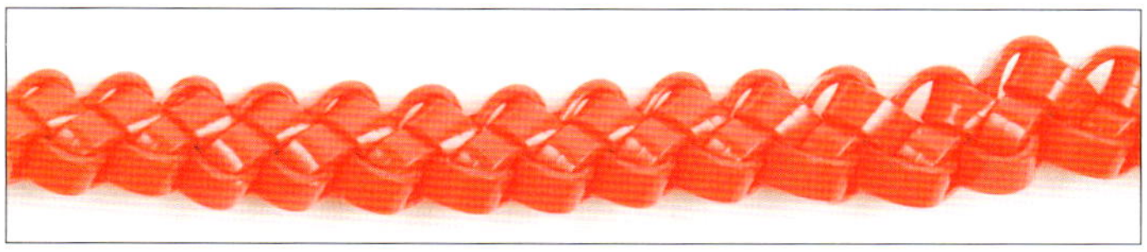

Slipper Braid

SIZE: 9"

MATERIALS for Bracelet:
Plastic 1/8" flat craft lace (6 feet of one color)

1. Fold the lace in half.

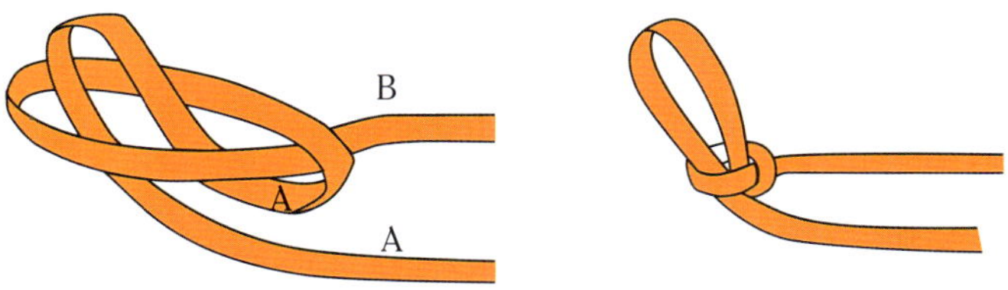

2. Bring A over B to form a loop.
3. Form part of A into a fold and push it into the loop.
   Pull B to form a Slip knot.

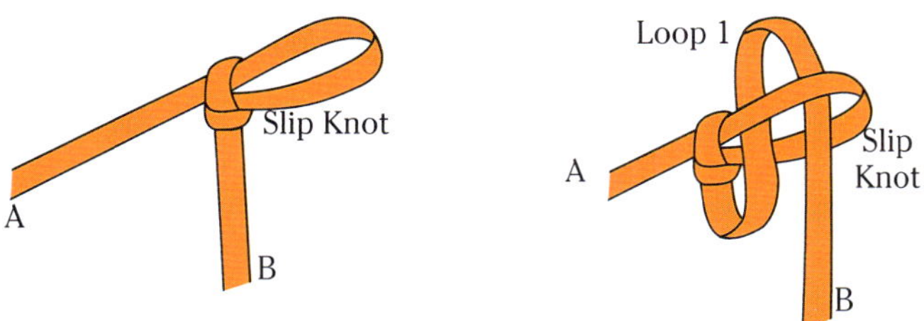

4. Gently pull A to adjust the size of the knot.
   Your Slip knot should look like this.
5. Push B into the Slip knot to form Loop 1.

6. Tighten the knot by firmly pulling on A.
   Push A into Loop 1 to form Loop 2.

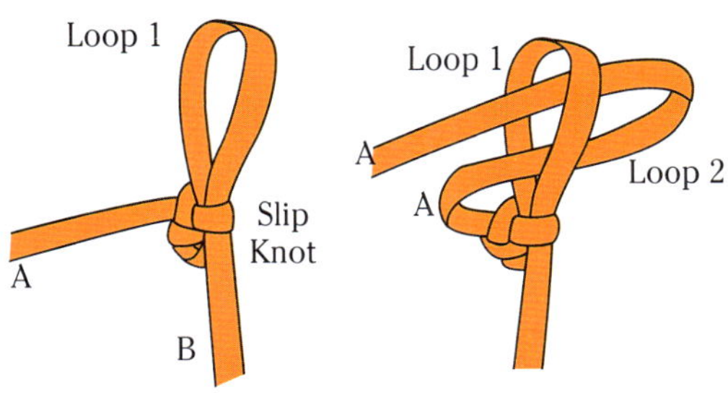

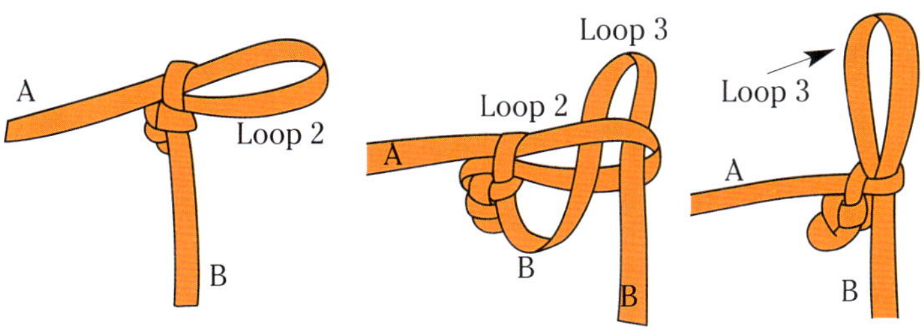

7. Tighten the knot by firmly pulling on B.
8. Push B into Loop 2 to form Loop 3.
9. Tighten the knot by firmly pulling on A.

10. Continue forming loops until the bracelet fits your wrist.
    Finish by forming a loop with strand A. Pull B tight.
11. Pull the end of A all the way out of the loop.

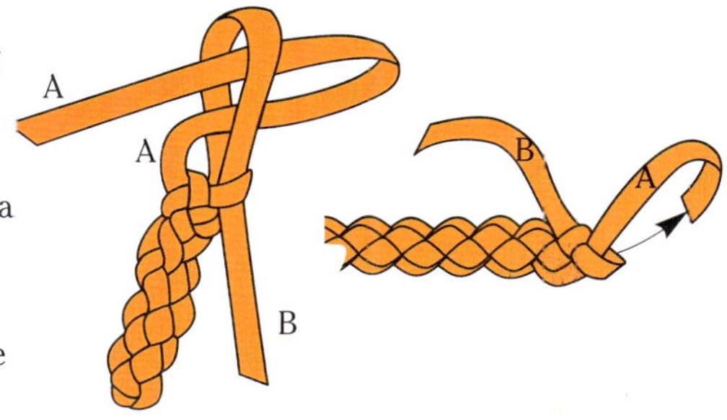

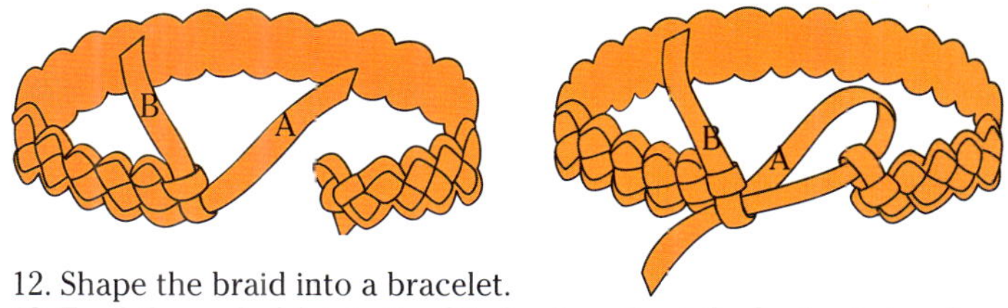

12. Shape the braid into a bracelet.
13. Feed the end of A into the Slip knot made at the beginning and thread A back into the loop for B.

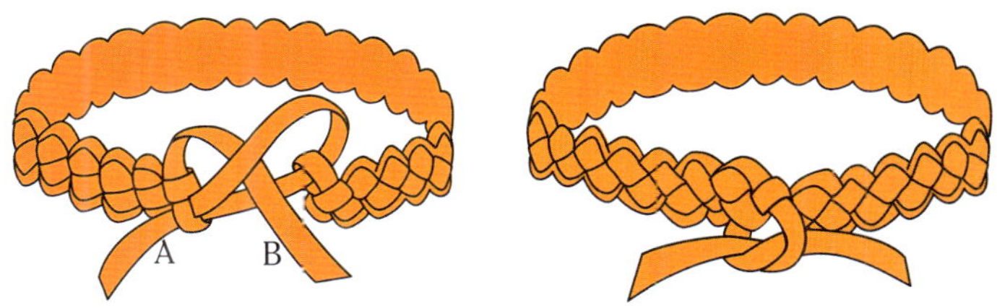

14. Push the end of B through the loop you just made with A.
15. Pull A and B to form a tight knot. Trim the tails.

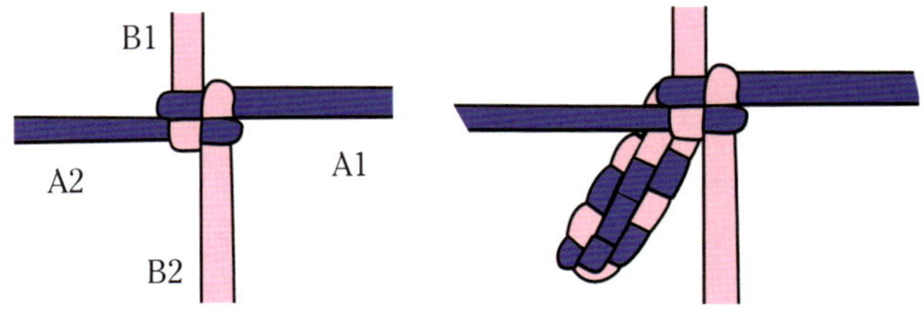

8. Pull all 4 laces tight to form the first 'square'.
9. Repeat steps 4 through 8 to form the second 'square' layer.

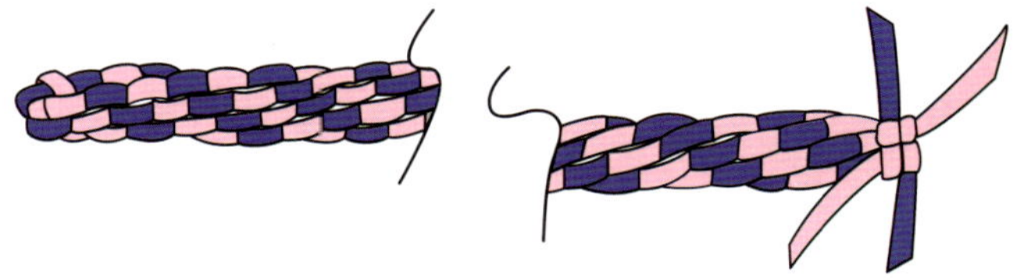

10. Continue braiding (keep braiding in the same direction, keep the laces flat, don't let the laces twist) repeating steps 4 through 8 until the bracelet fits your wrist.

The 'squares' will twist and spiral to form the cobra design.

Cobra Braid

SIZE: 9"

MATERIALS for Bracelet:

Plastic 1/8" craft lace (6 feet of Color A-Dark Blue, 6 feet of Color B-Pink)
Tape or Safety pin • Lanyard hook or paper clip

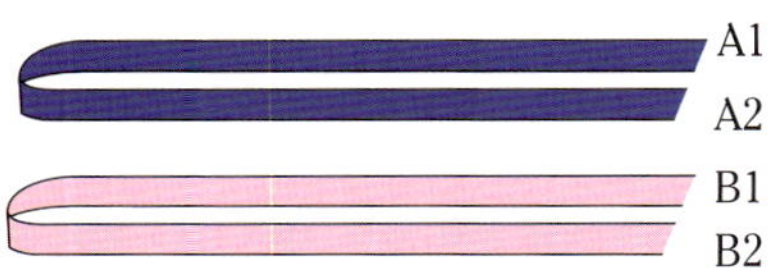

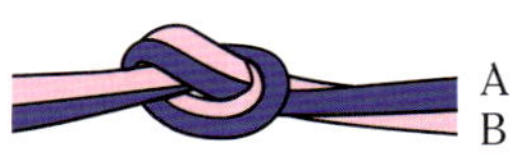

1. Cut the ends of each lace at an angle. Crease the middle.
2. Put strands together and attach a hook or paper clip to the fold. OR tie an Overhand knot at the fold. Tape or pin the hook to a surface to make it easier to braid.

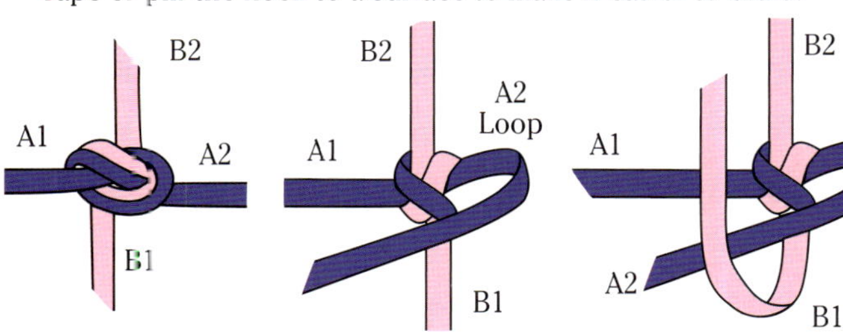

3. Position the laces as shown.
4. Bring A2 (form a loop) over B1.
5. Bring B1 over A2 and A1.

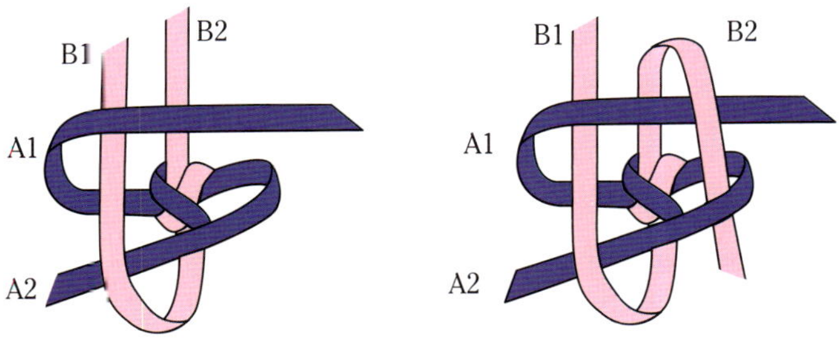

6. Bring A1 over B1 and B2.
7. Bring B2 over A1 and insert in the loop formed by A2.

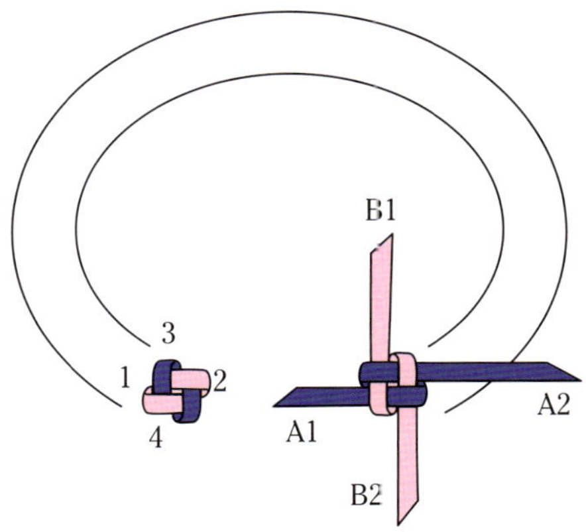

11. Remove the lanyard hook.
12. To make a circular bracelet, bend the Cobra Braid into a circle.

The ends should look like this.

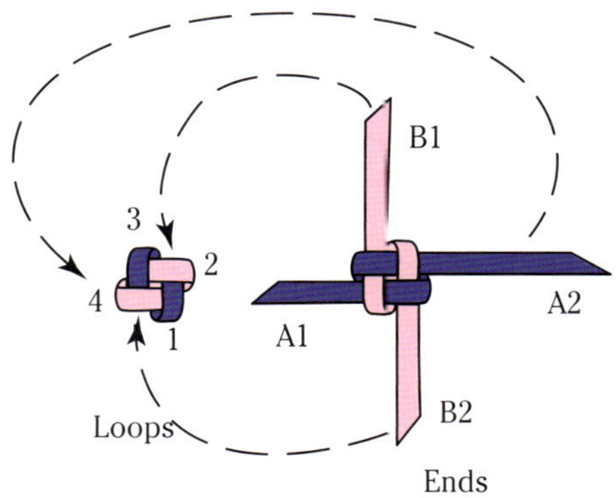

13. Slip the loose ends into the finished ends like this:
- Slip A1 through loop 1.
- Slip B1 through loop 2.
- Slip A2 through loop 3.
- Slip B2 through loop 4.

14. Pull all 4 ends tight to close the bracelet. Trim the loose ends.

KEYCHAIN: (36" of Color A-Dark Blue, 36" of Color B-Pink) Make a Cobra keychain by making the braid shorter and leaving the hook in place. Slip laces through a bead and add a dab of glue.

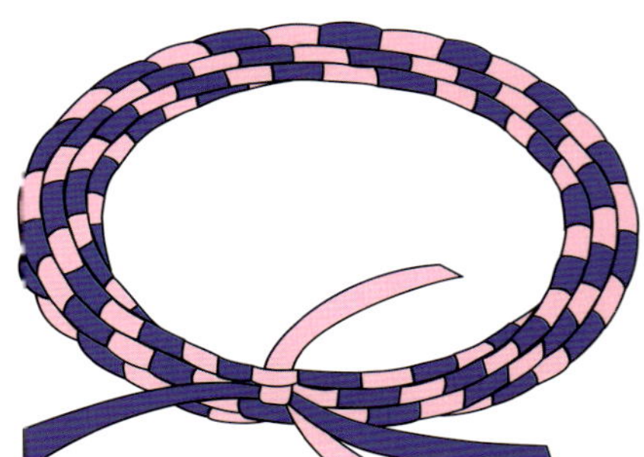

The Cobra Braid is also called the
4-Strand Spiral Braid

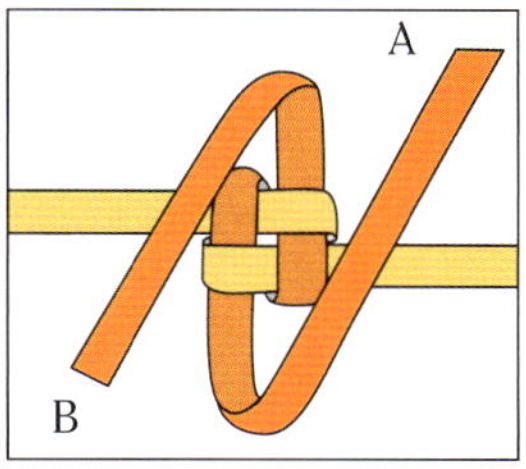

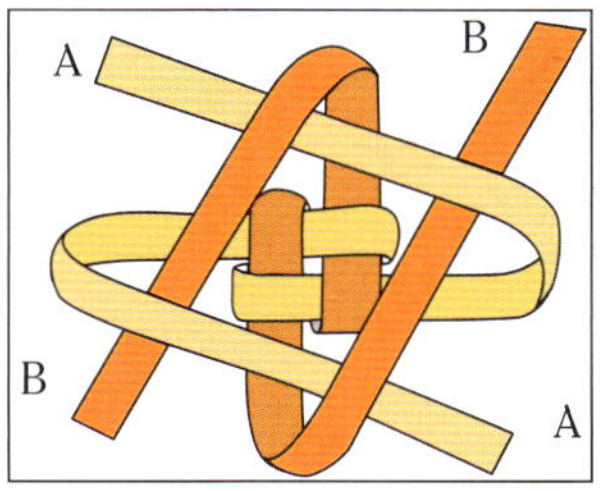

1. Make 1 row of square braid. Fold lace A up diagonally and lace A down diagonally across corners of square forming 2 loops.
2. Thread lace B over lace A and through bottom loop. Thread lace A over lace B and through the top loop.

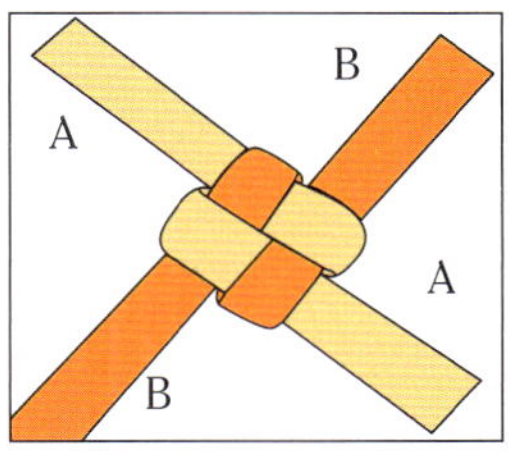

3. Pull ends forming a square. Continue making diagonal loops with laces A & A and bringing laces B & B over 1 lace and through loops. Laces A and A will alternate between top and bottom. Laces B and B will alternate between left and right sides.

Always fold laces diagonally across corners of square.

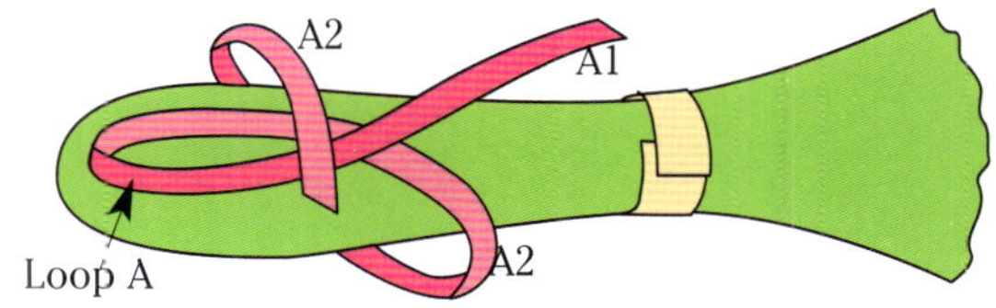

5. Tightly wrap A2 around the other laces.

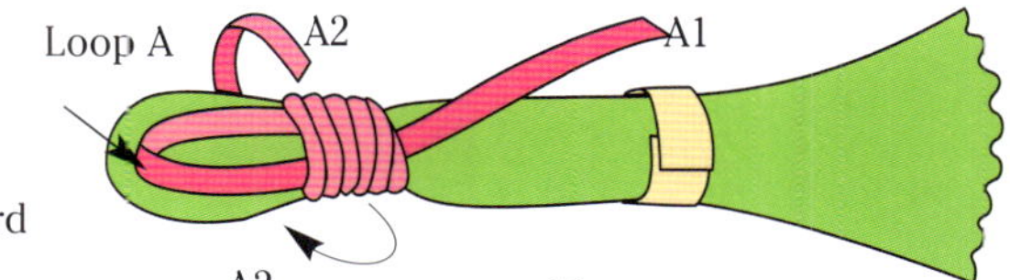

6. Continue wrapping A2 around the other laces, working toward the fold.

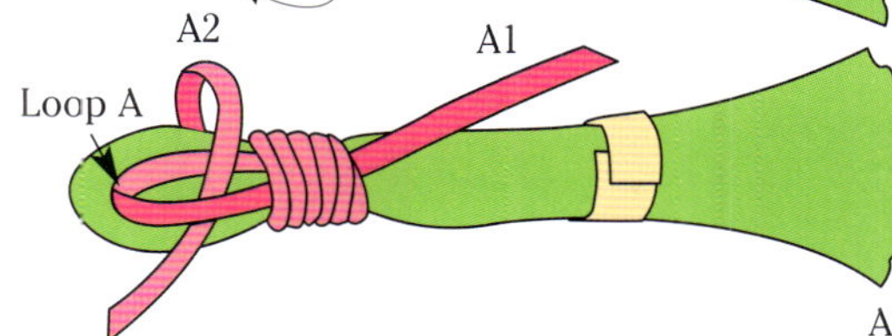

7. Pass A2 through Loop A.

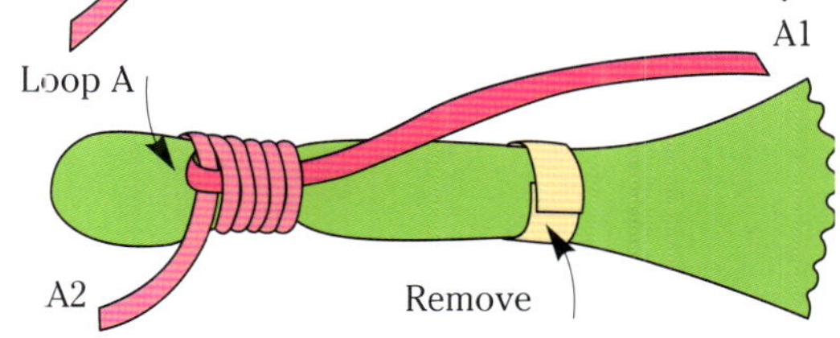

8. Tug gently on A1 until Loop A is drawn under the wraps.

Trim the ends evenly. Remove the tape.

Tassels

Tassels are great accents and make inexpensive gifts. Here's a fun way to use up leftover lace.

SIZE: 6"

MATERIALS:

1 piece of plastic 1/8" flat craft lace 24" long (Color A - Pink)

8 pieces of plastic 1/8" flat craft lace, each 10" long (Color B - Green)

Tape or Safety pin • Split Ring

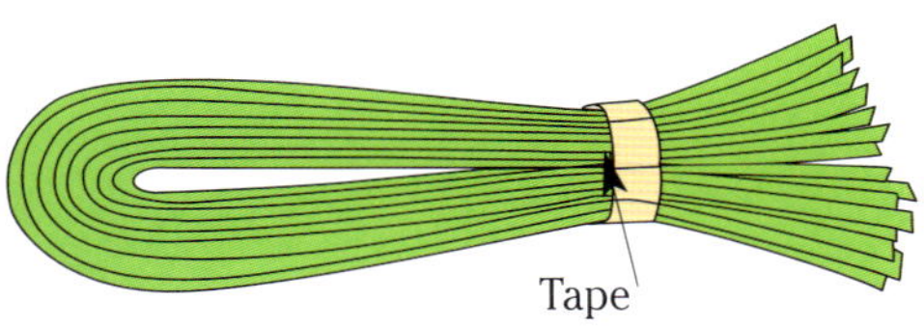

1. Stack the short laces together with ends even and fold in half.
2. Tape the laces together near the ends.

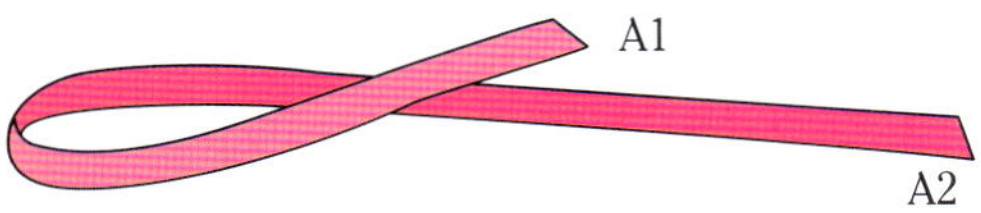

3. Label the long lace A. Fold A to make a loop.

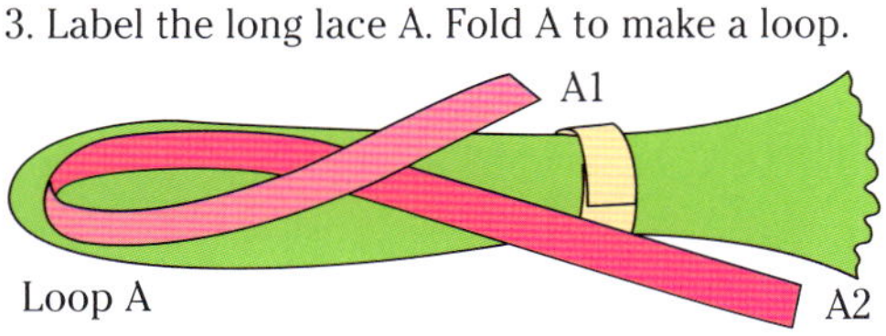

4. Place lace A over the taped laces as shown.

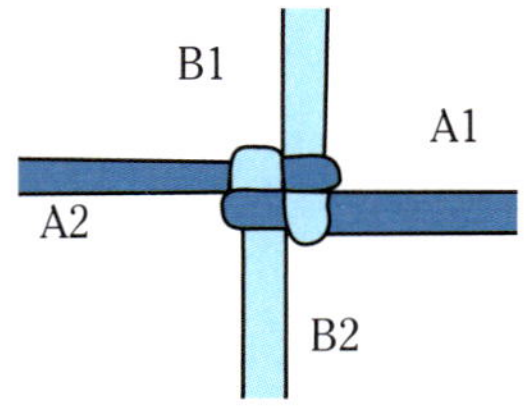

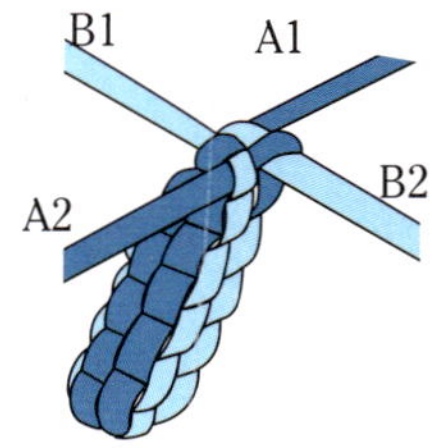

8. Keeping the laces flat, pull gently on all 4 strands to form a square.
9. Continue braiding until the lanyard reaches the desired length.
The A strands will always move horizontally and the B strands will move vertically. Remove the hook.
End with a Terminal Tie-Off.

Terminal Tie-off

This tie-off is used to End a Square or Spiral Braid

Leave the last row of braid loose. Working counter clockwise, bring each lace under the lace to the right of it and up through the center of braid.

When all four laces are through the center, tighten laces leaving tails below terminal tie-off.

KEYCHAIN: (36" of Color A-Red, 36" of Color B-Turquoise) Make a Box Stitch keychain by making the braid shorter. Slip a keyring onto B2 just before you close the circle. Join the ends to create a small 4" circle.

Box Stitch Braid

SIZE: 9"

MATERIALS for Bracelet:
Plastic 1/8' craft lace (6 feet of Color A-Dark Blue, 6 feet of Color B-Blue)
Tape or Safety pin • Lanyard hook or paper clip

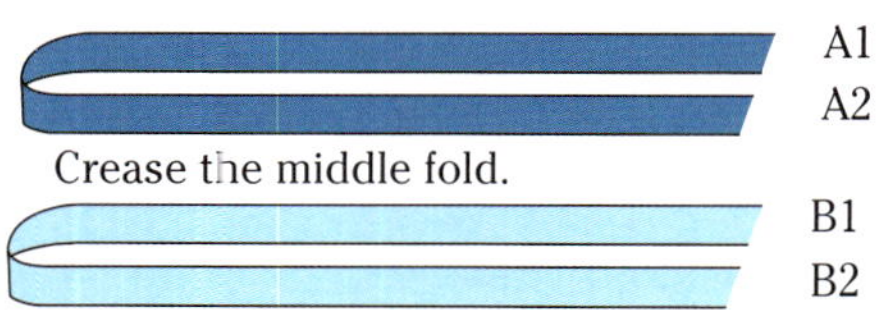

1. Cut the ends of each lace at an angle. Crease the middle.
2. Put strands together and attach a lanyard hook in the center with a tight Overhand knot.
Tape or pin the hook to a surface to make it easier to braid.

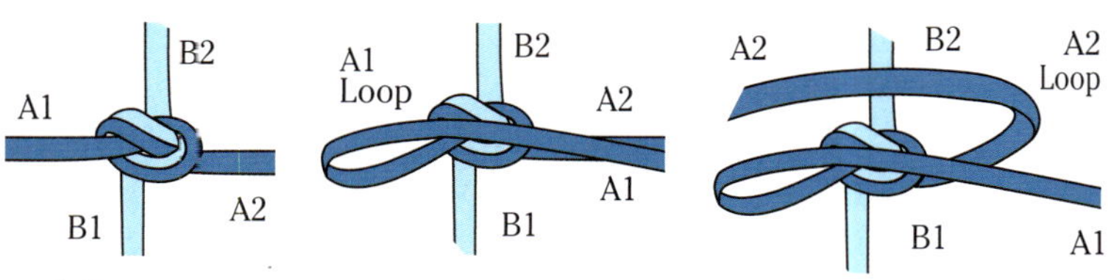

3. Position the laces as shown.
4. Fold A1 across (making a loop) to meet A2.
5. Fold A2 arcoss (making a loop) the front of B2.

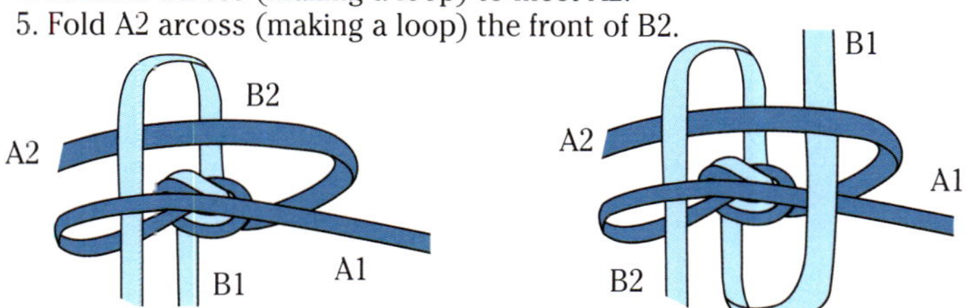

6. Fold B2 over A2 and through the loop formed by A1.
7. Slide B1 through the loop formed by A2.

The Box Stitch Braid is also called the 4-Strand Square Braid

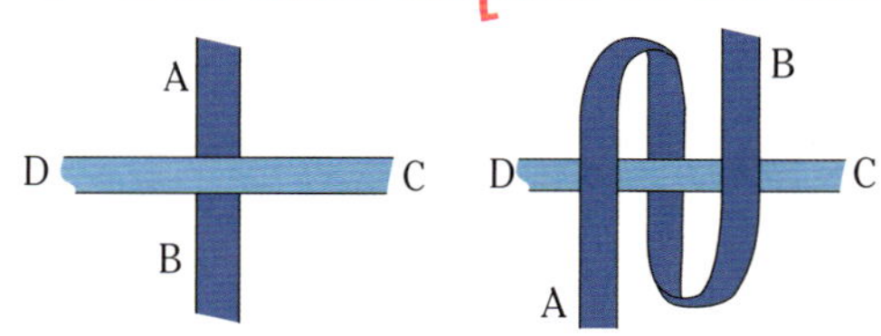

1. Thread the 2 laces of the same length through a split ring. Place split ring at the center of laces. Cross laces at center point. The split ring may be omitted if desired.
2. Fold lace A down to the left, fold lace B up to the right forming 2 loops.

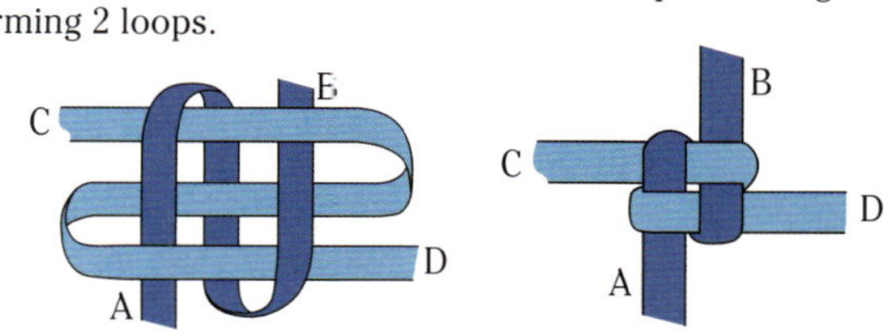

3. Thread lace C over lace B and through top loop. Thread lace D over lace A and through bottom loop.
4. Pull all 4 laces forming a tight square.
5. Continue making loops with vertical laces (A, B) and threading horizontal laces (C, D) over one lace and through loops. A and B will alternate between top and bottom. C and D will alternate between left and right sides. Always fold laces straight across square.
6. Repeat steps 2 - 5 until square braid is the required length. Tie off.

Diamond Braid

SIZE: 9"

MATERIALS for Bracelet:
Plastic 1/8" craft lace (36" of Color A-Dark Blue, 36" of Color B-Green)
Tape or Safety pin • Lanyard hook or paper clip

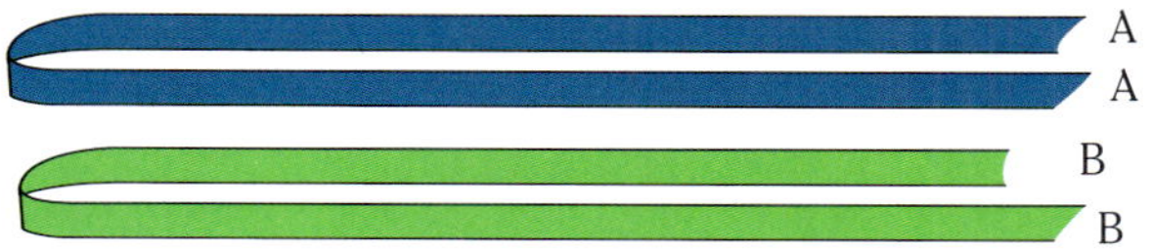

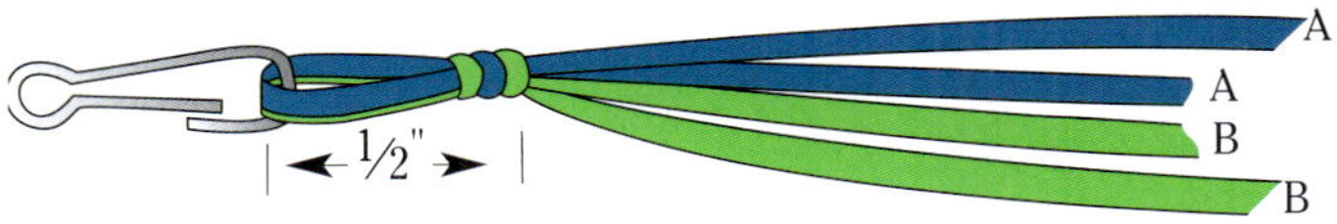

1. Fold each lace in half.
2. Attach a hook to the fold.
   Tie an Overhand knot 1/2" from the fold.

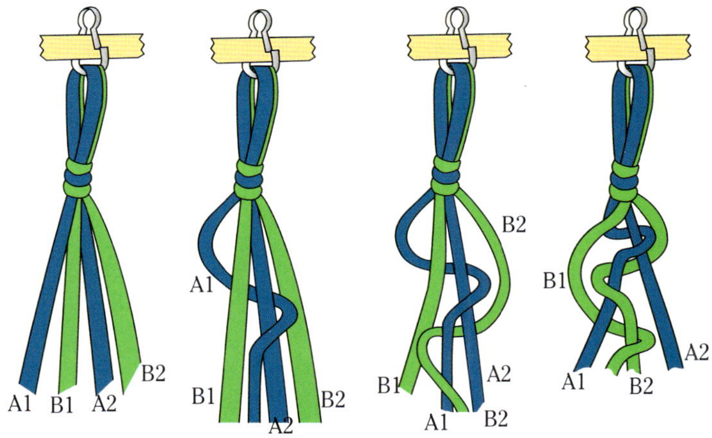

3. Tape or pin the hook to a surface to make it easier to braid.
   Arrange strands alternating the colors.
   (Tip: To create a different design, line up the strands A1-A2-B1-B2.)
4. Move A1 UNDER B1. Wrap under and AROUND A2.
5. Move B2 UNDER A2. Wrap under and AROUND A1.
6. Move B1 UNDER A1. Wrap under and AROUND B2.

7. After each step, pull tightly, keeping the strands flat.
   Do not allow the strands to twist.
   Continue until the bracelet fits your wrist.

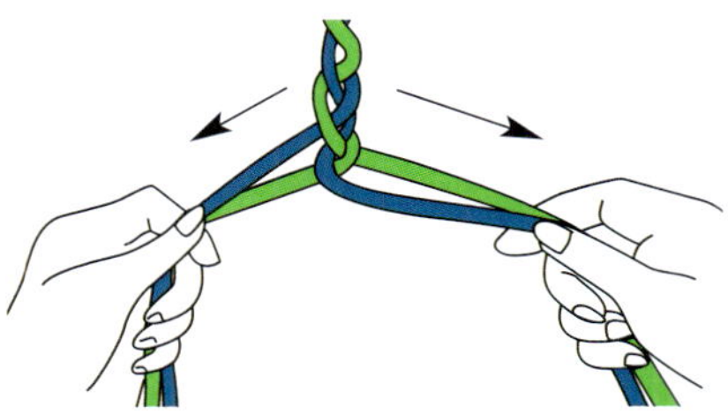

8. To finish, remove the tape and clip.
   Tie 2 Overhand knots, one on top of the other. Trim the tails.
   Wrap bracelet around your wrist and slide the knot into the loop.

KEYCHAIN: (18" of Color A-Dark Blue, 18" of Color B-Pink) Make a Diamond keychain by making the braid shorter and leaving the hook in place.

The Diamond Braid is also called the 4-Strand Round Braid

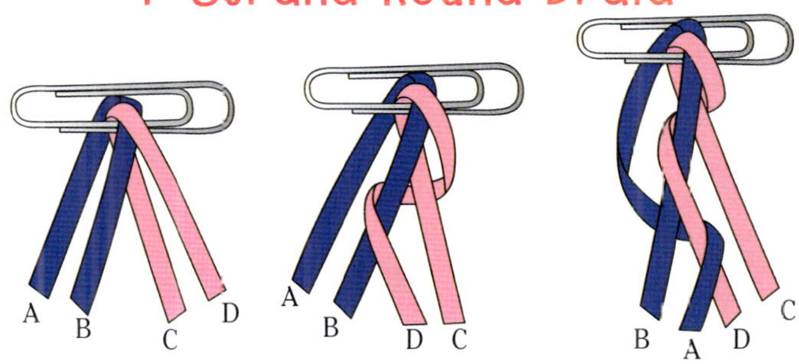

1. Thread 2 laces through a paper clip or lanyard hook and center with ends even. Position lace as in diagram.
2. Fold right outside lace D back, bring UNDER laces C and B, then fold forward OVER lace B.
3. Fold left outside lace A back, bring UNDER laces B and D, then fold forward OVER lace D.
4. Push laces tight.
   Continue to braid UNDER 2 and OVER 1, alternating the right and left outside laces.

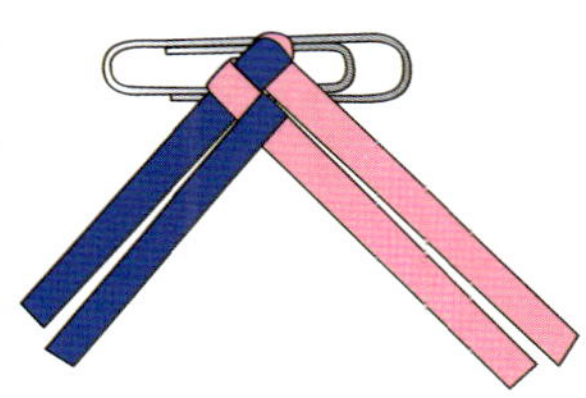

Dream Catcher

MATERIALS - SIZE: 6":
Plastic 1/8" craft lace (24 feet)
6" metal ring
Thunderbird nail head

Some Native American tribes believe dreams are messages sent by sacred spirits. There are many legends about dream catchers.

One is that the web captures good dreams while the bad dreams dissipate through the center hole. Another suggests that the web traps bad dreams to be destroyed by the morning light while allowing good dreams to pass through the center.

BASIC INSTRUCTIONS:

Use 12 feet of lace to cover a metal ring. Leaving an 8" tail, tape end of lace to ring. Wrap ring with lace covering it completely.

Leave an 8" tail. Remove tape and tie a knot against ring using the 2 lace ends. To make a hanger, bring lace ends together and tie an Overhand knot.

Use 12 feet of lace to make the web. Tie one end of lace to ring. Tie 12 half hitches around the ring. Space half hitches evenly with one exception, the space between last half hitch and beginning knot needs to be smaller. Pull lace tight as you work.

Tie a half hitch in center of first loop. Continue around web making half hitches in the center of each loop. Keep lace tight.

Secure lace with a knot near the center of web.

Cut off excess lace. Place a dab of jewelry glue on the knot.

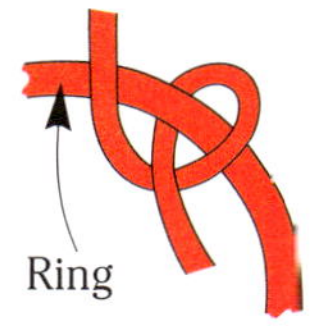

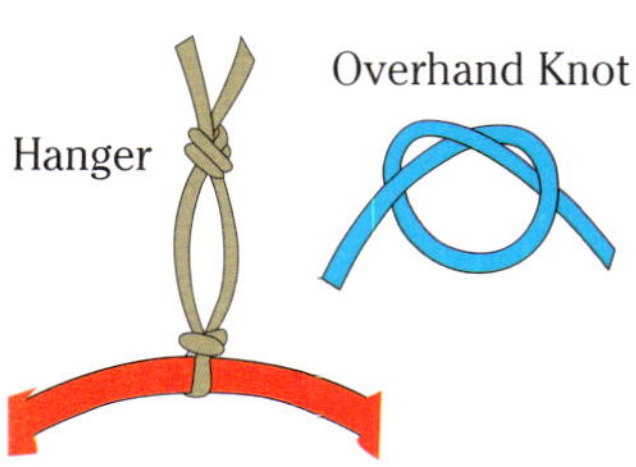

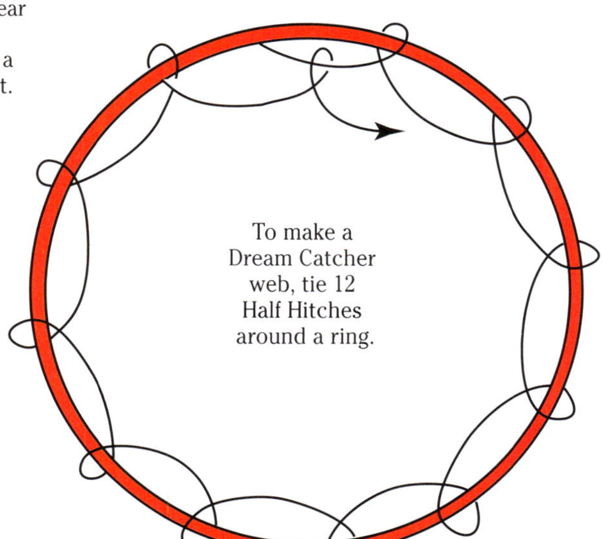

Neck Lanyard

SIZE: 18"
MATERIALS:
Plastic 1/8" flat craft lace (10 feet of Color A-Dark Blue, 10 feet of Color B-White)
Tape or Safety pin
Lanyard hook or paper clip

1. Fold the laces in half making the ends even.

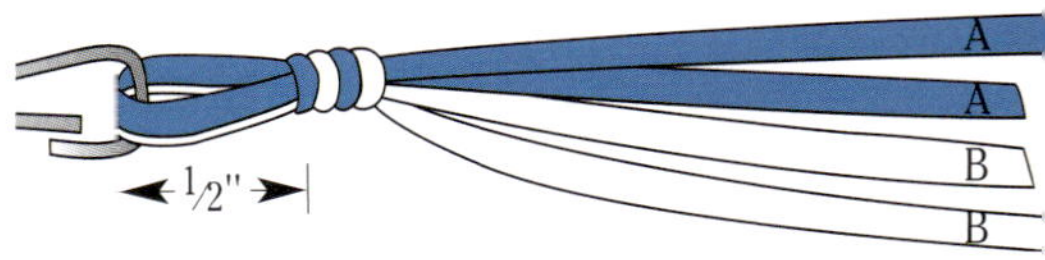

2. Attach a lanyard clip or safety pin to the fold. Tie an Overhand knot close to the fold. Tape or pin the hook to a surface to make it easier to braid.

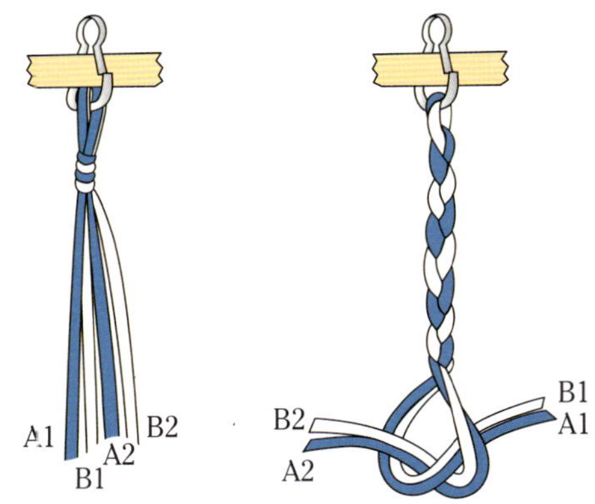

3. Arrange the strands in alternating colors. Follow the steps for the Diamond braid on page 11 (steps 4 through 6) until the braid is 3 feet long.
4. Hold A2 and B2 together. Hold A1 and B1 together. Tie the strands in a knot.

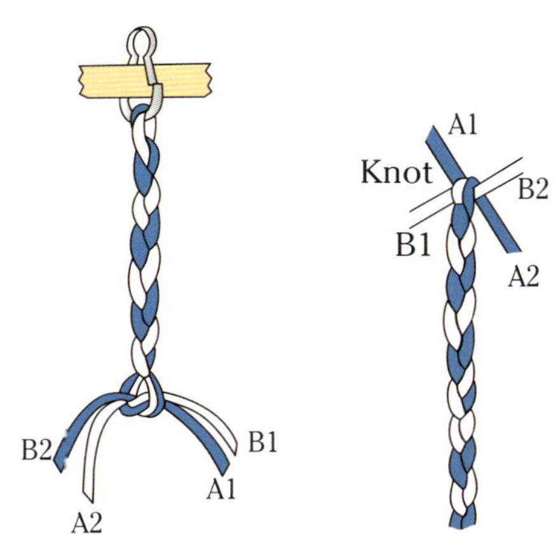

5. Tighten the knot to secure it.
6. Arrange the strands as shown. Move the pin to secure this knot to a surface.

Make a Large Box Stitch

Around the Diamond Braid to Make a Slip Knot

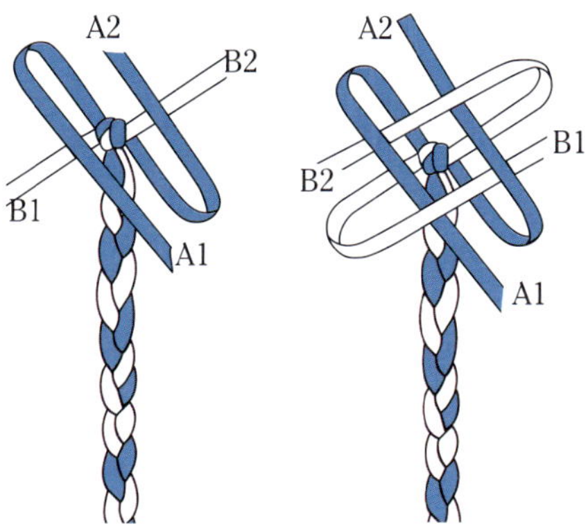

7. Begin the Box stitch by folding A1 over B1 and bringing A2 over B2.
8. Bring B2 over A2 and through the loop formed by A1. Bring B1 over A1 and through the loop formed by A2. Do not tighten yet.

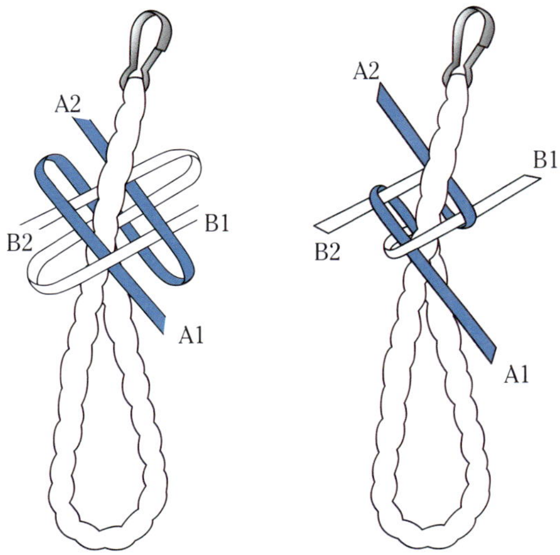

9. Remove the tape from the lanyard hook. Pass the hook through the center of the Box braid. When you pull 12" through the center of the box, the necklace loop will be 24".
10. Pull strands A1, A2, B1 and B2 tight.

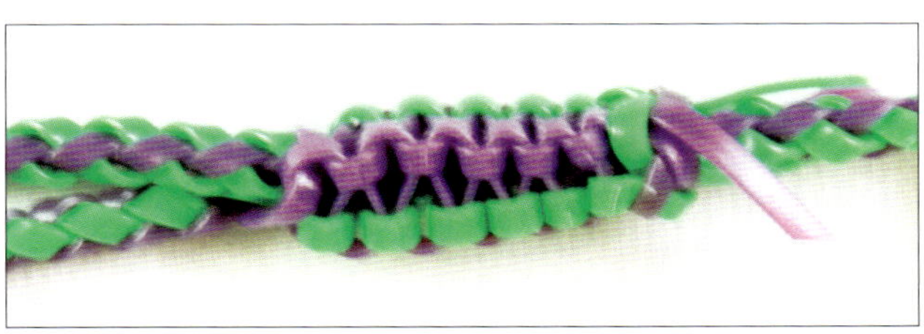

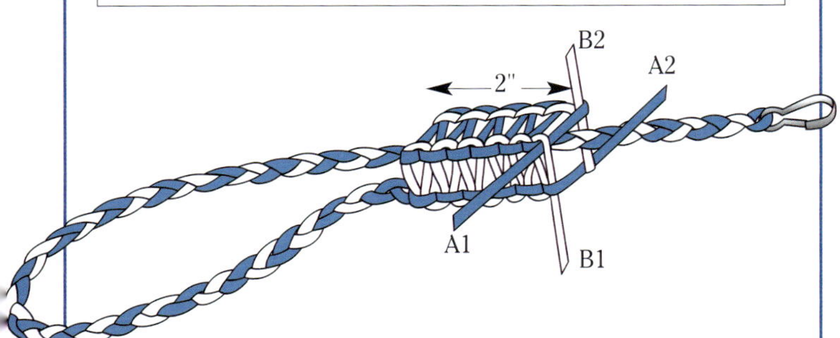

11. Continue the Box stitch for 2".
12. Follow the steps in the Finishing diagrams.

Finishing the Lanyard

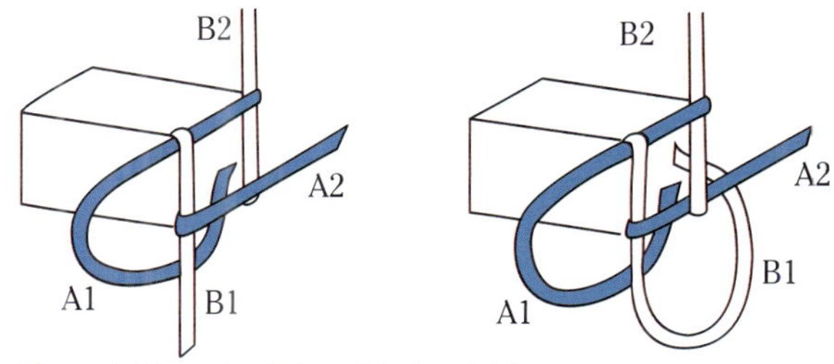

1. Thread A1 under B1 and behind A2.
2. Thread B1 behind A2 and B2.

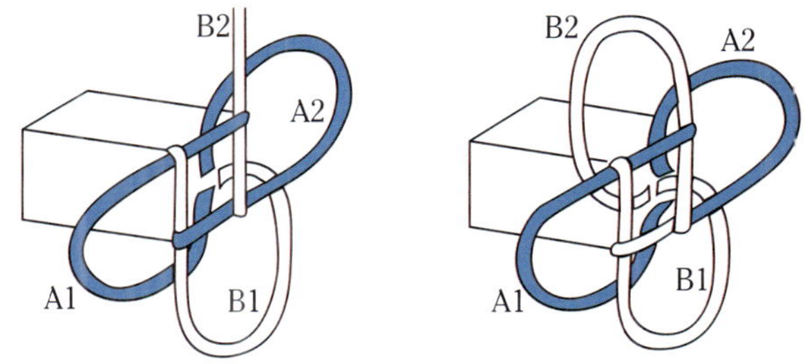

3. Thread A2 behind B2 and A1.
4. Thread B2 behind A1 and B1.

5. You now have 4 strand ends inside the box. Carefully pull one strand at a time to tighten. Apply a drop of Goop Adhesive to the end of the box. Let dry. Trim the loose ends.

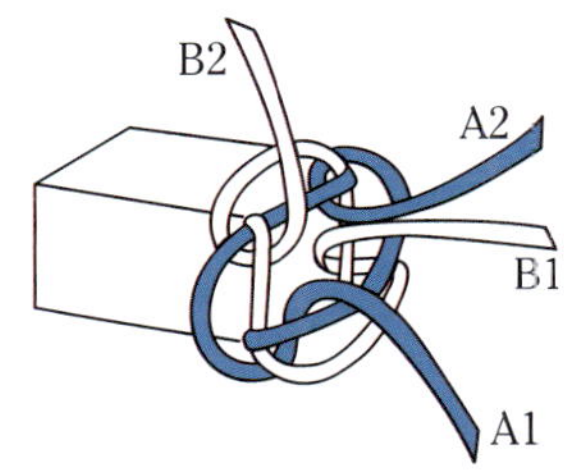

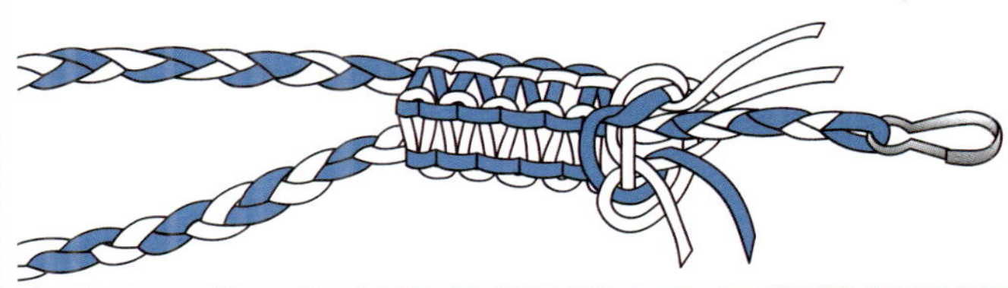

Short Lanyard Keychain

Here's a quick project that makes a great gift for Father's Day or Mother's Day.

SIZE: 5"

Plastic 1/8" craft lace (36" of Color A-Purple, 36" feet of Color B-Green)

Follow the Lanyard instructions with these changes:

1. Only braid 9" of the Diamond. Shorten the Box stitch to 1". Follow the Finishing steps above. Attach a split ring to the fold.

The Huichol Indians of Jalisco, Mexico create woven designs called Sikuli which means 'the power to see and understand things unknown.'

Ojos de Dios, or God's Eyes serve as a reminder that God is watching over us.

When a child is born, the central eye is woven by the father, then one eye is added for every year of the child's life until the child reaches the age of five.

Notch Dowels

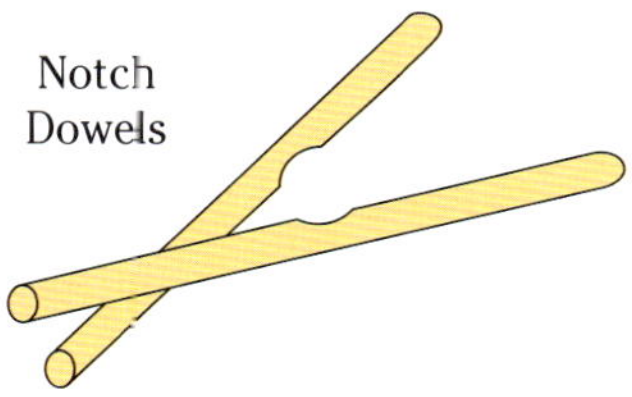

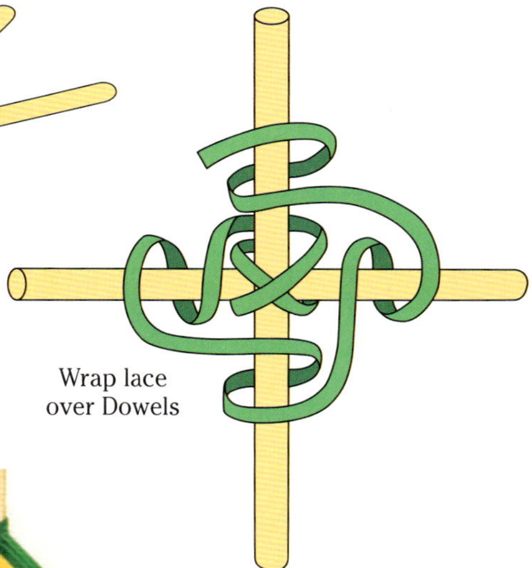

Wrap lace over Dowels

God's Eye Weavings

BASIC INSTRUCTIONS:

Use a craft knife to carefully notch the center of 2 dowels. Match notches and cross 1 dowel over the other. Wrap floral wire in an 'X' over the center of dowels.

Wrap lace over the center in an 'X'.

Wrap lace counter-clockwise over and around dowels forming a square. Do not twist lace. Pull tight. Push lace against previous wraps.

To change color, wrap the ending lace over dowel and tape to the underside. Tape beginning lace to underside of dowel and wrap lace up and over dowel. Wrap lace over and around the next dowel.

The ends will be secured as lace is wrapped around square.

To make a hanger, thread a piece of lace under wrapped lace at tip of a dowel. Bring ends together and tie an Overhand knot.

Small God's Eye

MATERIALS - SIZE: 3" x 3":
Plastic 1/8" craft lace (9 feet of Green, 8 feet of Yellow, 7 feet of Red)
Two 5" pieces of 3/8" dowel
26 gauge floral wire • Tape

INSTRUCTIONS:

Wrap lace in the following order: Green center, 3 rows Green, 3 rows Yellow, 3 rows Red, 2 rows Green, 2 rows Red, 4 rows Yellow, 3 rows Green.

Large God's Eye

MATERIALS - - SIZE: 8" x 8":
Plastic 1/8" craft lace (40 feet of Black, 17 feet of Turquoise, 15 feet of White, 13 feet of Red)
Two 10" pieces of 3/8" dowel
26 gauge floral wire • Tape

INSTRUCTIONS:

Wrap lace in the following order: Red center, 8 rows Red, 5 rows Black, 6 rows Turquoise, 3 rows Black, 4 rows White, 3 rows Black, 3 rows Red, 3 rows Black, 5 rows Turquoise, 3 rows Black, 2 rows White, 2 rows Black.

Flower Shapes on a Flower Wheel

Create simple and colorful flower shapes by wrapping lace around a special wheel.

MATERIALS - SIZE: 3" x 3" & 4" x 4":
Large and Small Flower Wheels
Large Flower -10 yards of 1/8" lace for flower, 2 yards of lace for center
Small Flower - 5 yards of 1/8" lace for flower, 1 yard of lace for center
Plastic tapestry needle

INSTRUCTIONS:
Hold the Wheel with the letters facing you, A at the top.
Using the longest lace, wrap around A, and follow the chart:

Bottom Pegs Go to the Right	Top Pegs Go to the Left
Peg F	Peg E
Peg D	Peg C
Peg B*	Peg A
Peg F	Peg E
Peg D	Peg C
Peg B*	repeat

This completes 1 round.

Repeat for 4 to 5 rounds.

Weave the end into the back of the flower to secure.

Using the short lace, weave the end into the back of the flower to secure it.

Bring the lace to the front of the flower.

Pass over 2 and under 1 loop, going around until your center has reached the desired size.

Weave the end under the flower in the back to secure.

Trim excess lace as needed and remove flower from wheel.

Apply a drop of glue to the lace ends if desired.

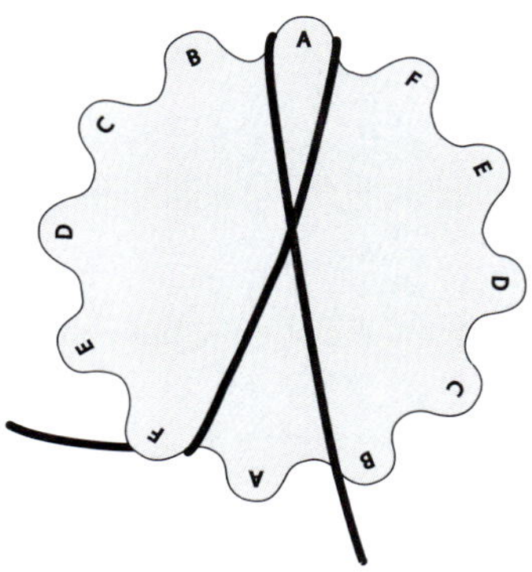

Begin by wrapping A to F.

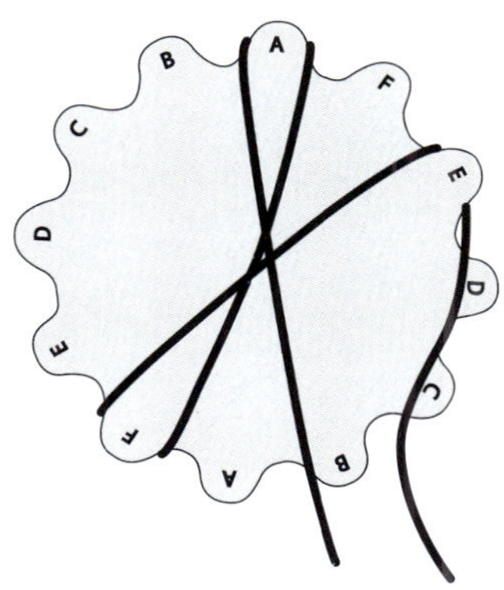

Continue around E, D, C, etc.

Pass over 2 and under 1 around the center.

Make Easy Bracelets with a Braiding Wheel

You're going to love weaving simple bracelets with a Weaving Wheel. Position colors to create interesting patterns. Combine floss colors with yarns and beads to add interesting textures. Designs will vary depending on the quantity and position of the colors at set-up. Have fun!

Braiding Wheels

Purchase a Wheel - An inexpensive foam wheel (from Toner Plastics) is available at craft shops in the plastic lace department.

Note: A thick 'foam' wheel holds floss firmly between the sections. It works much better than a cardboard wheel.

see pages 16 - 17 for braiding instructions

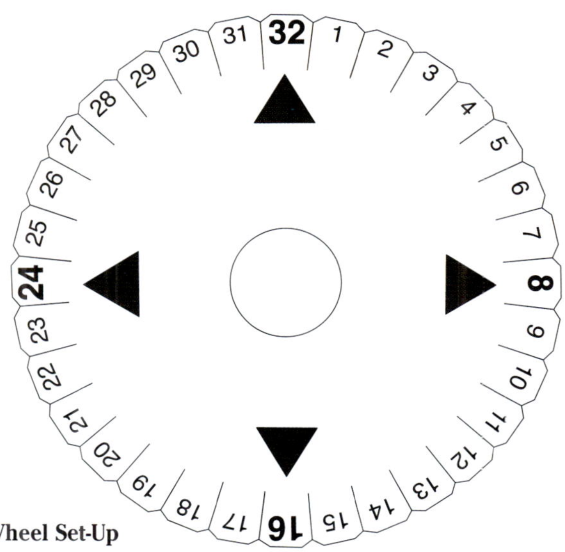

Braiding Wheel Set-Up

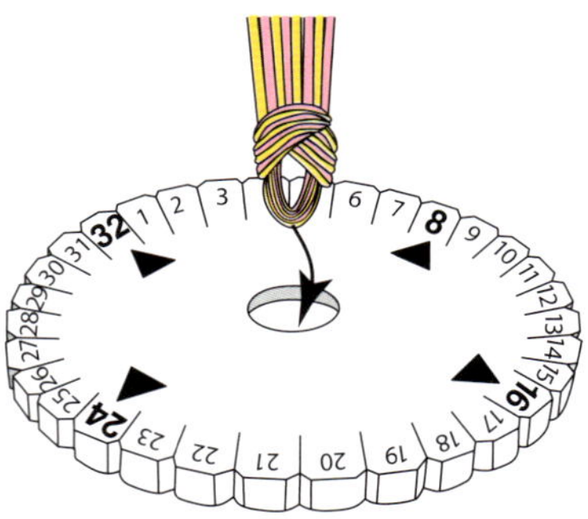

Braiding with a Wheel

You can easily braid colorful cords with an inexpensive foam wheel.

SIZE: 6"

BASIC MATERIALS:
Plastic 1/8" craft lace
(2 each - 80" of Color A, 2 each - 80" of Color B)
Weaving Wheel (with 32 slots) - see page 15
1 lanyard hook or safety pin

BASIC INSTRUCTIONS:
Slide all strands through a lanyard hook.
Fold strands in half with the hook at the fold.
Tie an Overhand knot to keep the hook in place.
Place hook through the center of the wheel.
Set up the cords for the desired design.

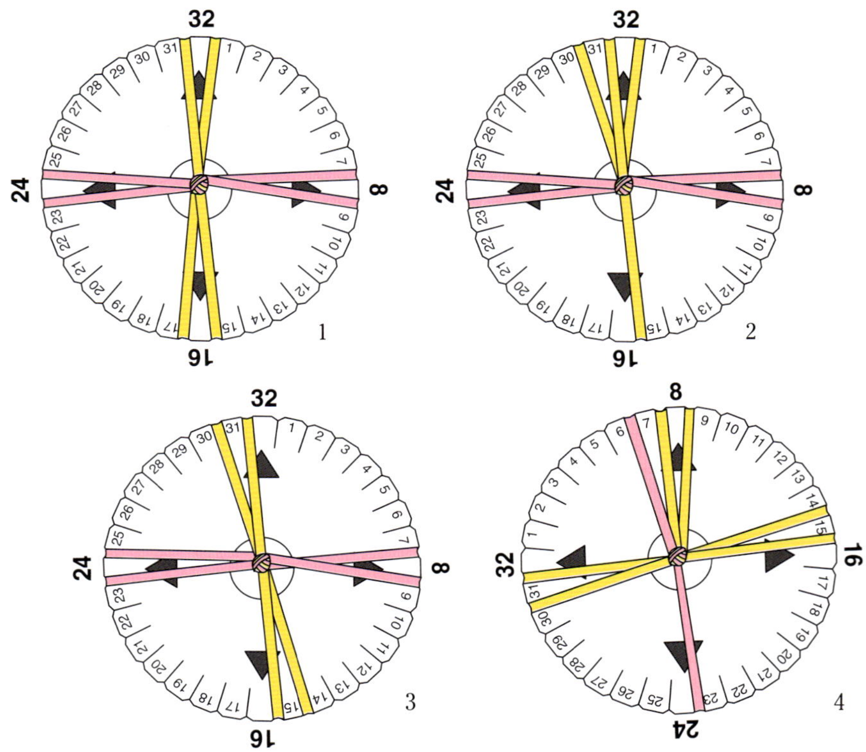

Round Braid #1

INSTRUCTIONS: In this style of braid, the numbers change as the wheel rotates.

Begin with #32 at the Top.

1. Always start with the bottom left strand (between 16 & 17) and place it to the left of the top strands (between 30 & 31).
2. There are now 3 strands on top.
3. Pull out the right strand at the top (between 1 & 32) and insert it to the right of the bottom strands (between 14 & 15).

Turn the Wheel Counterclockwise.

4. Pick up the bottom left lace (between 24 & 25) and place it in the slot to the left of the top lace (between 6 & 7).

Pick up the top right lace (between 8 & 9) and place it in the slot to the right of the bottom lace (between 22 & 23).

Turn the Wheel Counterclockwise.

Repeat until you reach the desired length. (Note: This step is not illustrated).
Remove the lanyard from the wheel and knot the ends together.

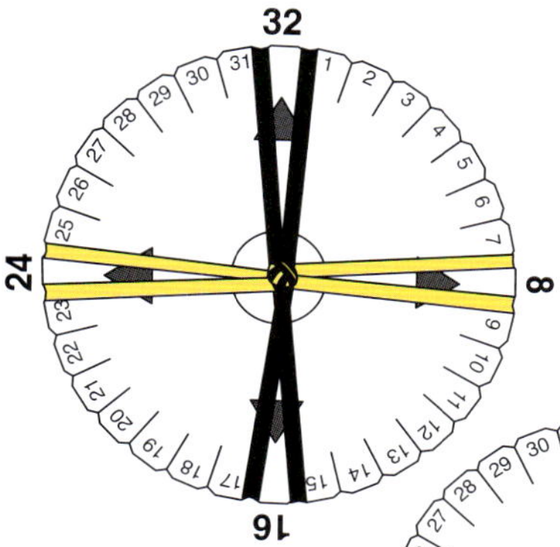

Flat Braid #2

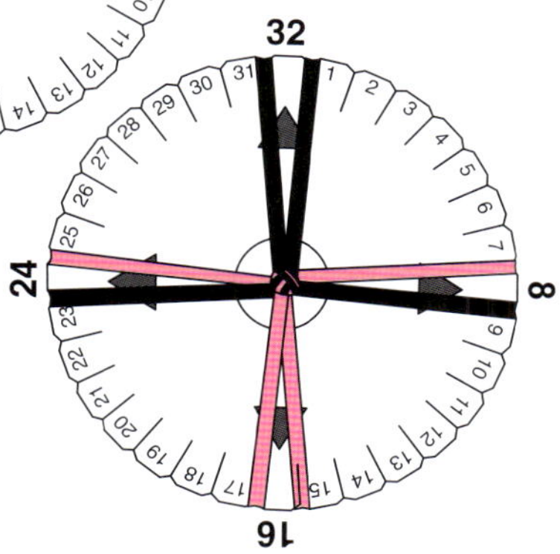

Flat Braid #3

Flat Braid #2 - #3

INSTRUCTIONS:

Step A:
Move lace between 31 & 32 and insert between 9 & 10.
Move lace between 32 & 1 and insert between 22 & 23.
Move lace between 16 & 17 and insert between 6 & 7.
Move lace between 15 & 16 and insert between 25 & 26.

Step B:
Move lace between 7 & 8 and insert between 15 & 16.
Move lace between 24 & 25 and insert between 16 & 17.
Move lace between 8 & 9 and insert between 32 & 1.
Move lace between 23 & 24 and insert between 31 & 32.

Step C:
Move lace between 6 & 7 and insert between 7 & 8.
Move lace between 9 & 10 and insert between 8 & 9.
Move lace between 25 & 26 and insert between 24 & 25.
Move lace between 22 & 23 and insert between 23 & 24.
Repeat Steps A, B & C until you reach the desired length.

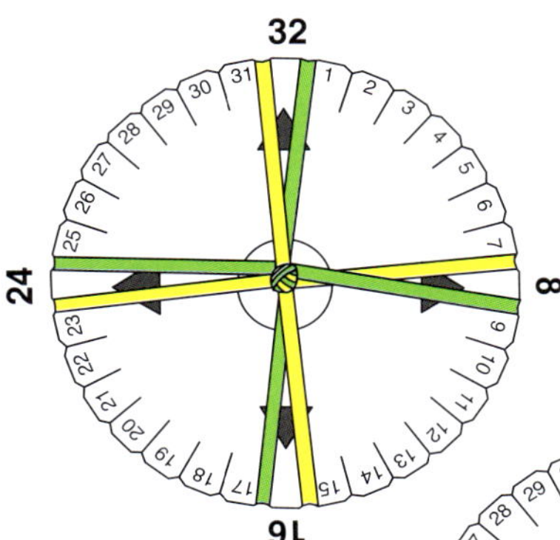

Rectangular Braid #4

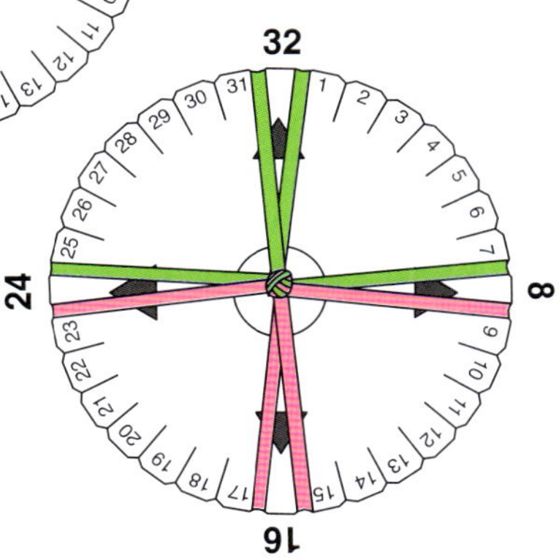

Rectangular Braid #5

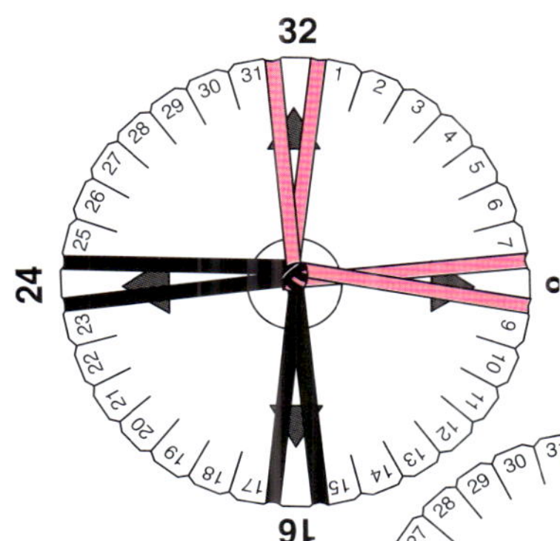

Square Braid #6

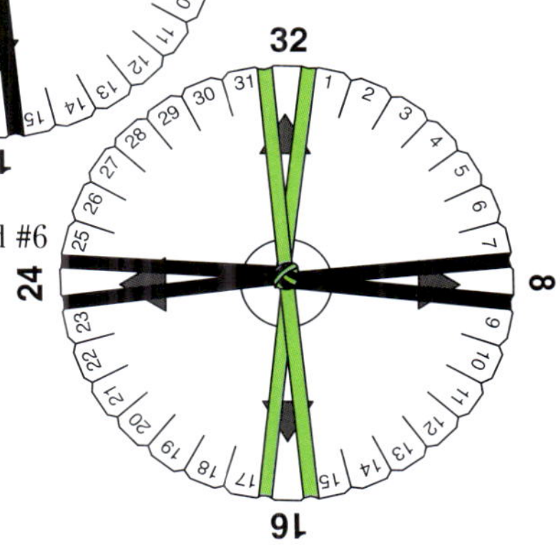

Square Braid #7

Rectangular Braid #4 - #5

INSTRUCTIONS:

Step A:
Move lace between 32 & 1 and insert between 1 & 2.
Move lace between 15 & 16 and insert between 32 & 1.
Move lace between 1 & 2 and insert between 15 & 16.

Step B:
Move lace between 24 & 25 and insert between 25 & 26.
Move lace between 23 & 24 and insert between 22 & 23.
Move lace between 7 & 8 and insert between 24 & 25.
Move lace between 8 & 9 and insert between 23 & 24.
Move lace between 25 & 26 and insert between 7 & 8.
Move lace between 22 & 23 and insert between 8 & 9.

Step C:
Move lace between 31 & 32 and insert between 30 & 31.
Move lace between 16 & 17 and insert between 31 & 32.
Move lace between 30 & 31 and insert between 16 & 17.
Repeat Steps A, B & C until you reach the desired length

Square Braid #6 - #7

INSTRUCTIONS:

Step A:
Move lace between 32 & 1 and insert between 6 & 7.
Move lace between 16 & 17 and insert between 22 & 23.
Move lace between 23 & 24 and insert between 32 & 1.
Move lace between 7 & 8 and insert between 16 & 17.

Step B:
Move lace between 15 & 16 and insert between 9 & 10.
Move lace between 31 & 32 and insert between 25 & 26.
Move lace between 24 & 25 and insert between 15 & 16.
Move lace between 8 & 9 and insert between 31 & 32.

Step C:
Move lace between 6 & 7 and insert between 7 & 8.
Move lace between 9 & 10 and insert between 8 & 9.
Move lace between 25 & 26 and insert between 24 & 25.
Move lace between 22 & 23 and insert between 23 & 24.
Repeat Steps A, B & C until you reach the desired length.

Suzanne McNeill

Suzanne has been designing crafts and creating fresh ideas for all ages for over 25 years.

She shares her creativity in books by Design Originals.

The popular best-selling books are known for simple and colorful designs.

Her mission is to publish books that help others learn about the best projects, newest techniques and most popular products.

Supplier

Most craft stores carry an excellent assortment of supplies. If you need something special, ask your local store to contact the following company.

CRAFT LACE
WEAVE WHEEL
FLOWER WHEEL

Toner Plastics
www.tonercrafts.com

MANY THANKS to my staff for their cheerful help and wonderful ideas!

Kathy Mason
Kristy Krouse
Patty Williams
Donna Kinsey
David & Donna Thomason

Braided Bracelet

SIZE: 9"

MATERIALS:
Plastic 1/8" flat craft lace (22" of Color A-Turquoise, 18" of Color B-Pink, 18" of Color C-Dark Blue)
Tape or Safety pin • Lanyard hook or paper clip

1. Put strands together and fold a 4" Color A-Turquoise loop at one end. Slip a lanyard hook onto the loop.

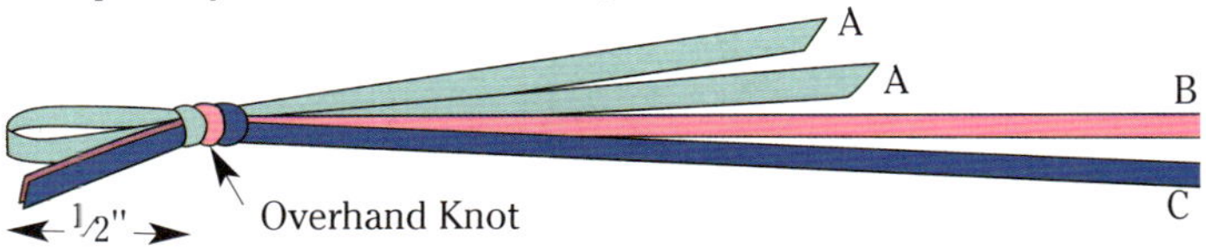

2. Tie an Overhand knot 1/2" from the fold. Tape or pin the hook to a surface to make it easier to braid.
3. Spread the strands and position them as shown.
4. Bring C over B.
5. Bring A over C.
Tighten and repeat to fit your wrist.
6. Tie 2 Overhand knots, one on top of the other. Trim the tails.

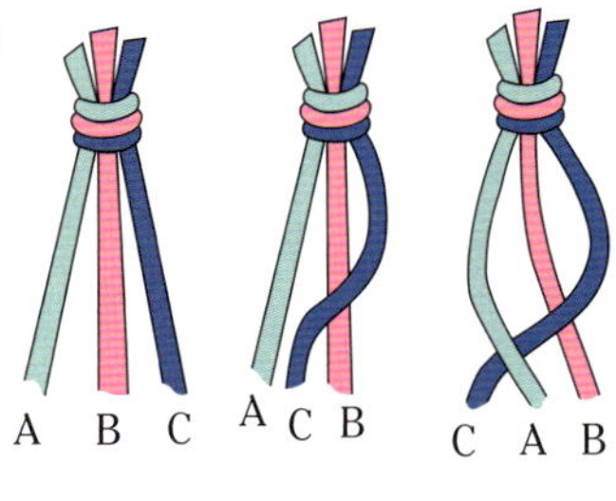

Twisted Hitch Bracelet

SIZE: 9"

MATERIALS:
Plastic 1/8" craft lace
(34" of Color A-Yellow, 30" of Color B-Pink, 30" of Color C-Green)
Tape or Safety pin • Lanyard hook or paper clip

1. Put strands together and fold a 4" Color A-Yellow loop at one end. Slip a lanyard hook onto the loop.
2. Tie an Overhand knot 1/2" from the fold (see illustration above). Tape or pin the hook to a surface to make it easier to braid.
3. Spread the strands and position them as shown.

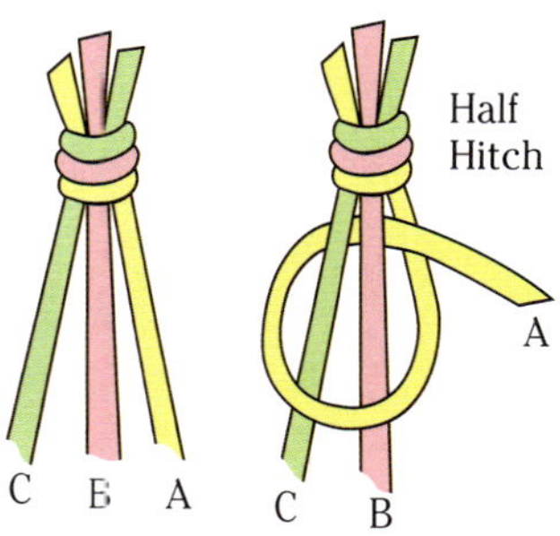

4. The Half Hitch is simple, just wrap one strand around another.
5. Make 8 Half Hitches with Color A-Yellow. (The knots will form a corkscrew-like spiral).
6. Switch colors and make 8 Half Hitches with Color B-Pink.
7. Switch colors and make 8 Half Hitches with Color C-Green.
Repeat steps 4 - 6 to fit your wrist.
8. Tie 2 Overhand knots, one on top of the other. Trim the tails.

Purple & Turquoise Bracelet

SIZE: 9 1/2"

MATERIALS:
Plastic canvas (7 count), 5 squares x 61 squares
Plastic 1/8" craft lace
(7 feet of Color A-Turquoise, 16 feet of Color B-Purple)

INSTRUCTIONS:
1. Shape canvas into a bracelet, overlapping 4 squares on the ends. Thread lace up through the lapped ends of canvas.

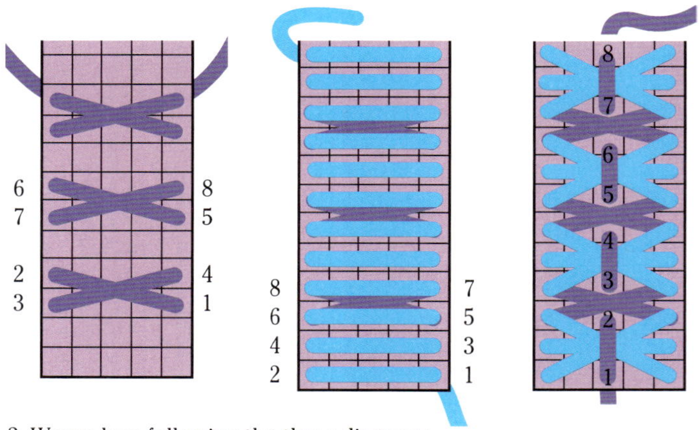

2. Weave lace following the three diagrams.

Loop Stitch

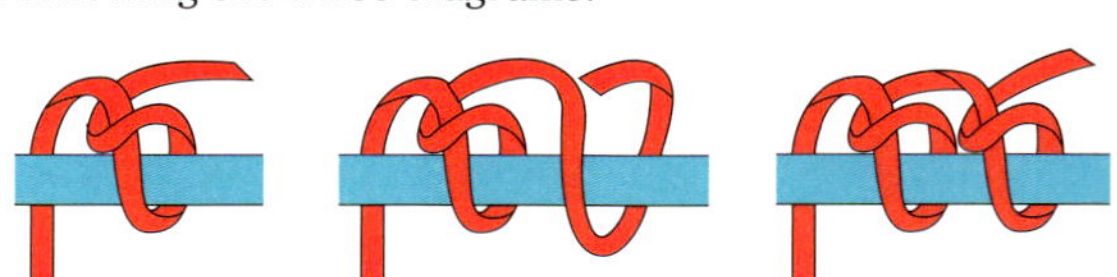

3. Finish edges with a Loop stitch. Cut lace 5 1/2 times the length to be stitched. Temporarily anchor lace in the 1st canvas square.
4. Bring lace over the edge and down through 2nd square forming a loop. Bring end over edge and back through the 1st loop. Grasp the 2nd loop and pull the 1st loop tight.
5. Pull the second loop tight. Stitch along the entire edge, returning to the starting point. (TIP: Place 2 stitches in each corner square).
6. Pull beginning lace out of the first square. Place a stitch in the first square. Bring lace over edge, thread down through first loop and first square. Weave ends under the stitches on the wrong side.